A – M

BY JANE ELLING HAAS

ILLUSTRATED BY CAROLYN BRAUN

SAINT LOUIS

This book is affectionately dedicated to my husband, Don, and to our daughters, Emily and Bethany, with whom I've been blessed to share many celebrations as a Christian family; and to all educators in Christ's family who share the faith and celebrate with joy what God does for us each day!

(Philemon 1:4–7)

Scripture quotations taken from the HOLY BIBLE, NEW INTERNATIONAL VERSION®. NIV®. Copyright © 1973, 1978, 1984 by International Bible Society. Used by permission of Zondervan Publishing House. All rights reserved.

Copyright © 1998 Concordia Publishing House
3558 S. Jefferson Avenue, St. Louis, MO 63118-3968
Manufactured in the United States of America

Teachers who purchase this product may reproduce pages for use in parish-education programs.

All rights reserved. Except as noted above, no part of this publication may be reproduced, stored in a retrieval system, or transmitted, in any form or by any means, electronic, mechanical, photocopying, recording, or otherwise, without the prior written permission of Concordia Publishing House.

1 2 3 4 5 6 7 8 9 10   07 06 05 04 03 02 01 00 99 98

Contents

Introduction 4
Celebrate **A**postles .6
Celebrate **B**aptism 10
Celebrate **C**reation 14
Celebrate **D**eath and Resurrection 20
Celebrate **E**aster .24
Celebrate **F**orgiveness 28
Celebrate **G**ospel 32
Celebrate **H**eaven 36
Celebrate **I**nheritance 40
Celebrate **J**esus .44
Celebrate **K**ingdom 48
Celebrate **L**eaders 52
Celebrate **M**usic 55
Patterns 58

INTRODUCTION

WHAT IS A CELEBRATION CENTER?

A celebration center is where one person or a group of people come together to do one or more activities related to a Bible lesson in celebration of God's grace.

This book of ideas is designed to help you make and use hands-on activities with children in grades 3 to 5. The ideas also work well in intergenerational settings where adults and children can work together. You may use these ideas in Sunday, midweek, or day school settings; in family night celebrations at church; and in homeschooling and family devotion settings.

WHAT YOU WILL FIND INSIDE

This book provides themes listed alphabetically for the *first half* of the alphabet. For each theme, you will find the following:

- Suggestions for Scripture readings
- Bible stories to learn
- Special Bible verses to read and remember
- Suggested books to read
- Activities and directions to help reinforce the Scripture focus
- Illustrations and suggested materials to help you set up and prepare for the center and its activities
- Directions for each activity and patterns when appropriate

FIVE REASONS TO USE CELEBRATION CENTERS

1. Celebration centers emphasize learning by doing, touching, and using the five senses.
2. Centers invite interaction among learners of various age levels and between students and leaders.
3. Centers provide a change of pace for learning experiences from a traditional classroom approach.
4. Celebration centers encourage learners of all ages to read the Bible, share Bible stories, and reinforce their learning through daily life applications.
5. Centers complement lessons by providing opportunity to expand activities, discover new facts and relationships, and make concrete life applications.

Six Ways to Use Celebration Centers

1. Set up celebration centers in day school classrooms as additional activities for students to complete as time and space allow.
2. Engage in celebration centers as a supplement to a home-school curriculum.
3. Use center ideas as a supplement to your regular Sunday morning educational program. Teachers might direct a "center" room during the first or last 30 minutes of Sunday school or midweek school for all ages, including adults. Activities can reinforce what learners hear during their regular lesson time.
4. Create learning centers on special Sundays of the church year, in various seasons, or at any time that you want to provide intergenerational activities.
5. Invite all ages to participate in learning activities together during school vacations and use one or more classrooms for designing celebration centers. Encourage people to bring friends and neighbors as a way of reaching more with the Gospel.
6. Make celebration centers at home to do together as families. Invite friends and neighbors. Use center ideas in "cell" Bible study groups.

How to Use This Book

Read through each center entirely. The center setup is only one of several possibilities for how to present the theme and activities. Make adjustments according to your setting. Keep in mind that the books listed in the **Books to Read** section are not the only ones available on the theme. If working with older children, you will want to include books and Bible story collections at their reading level.

As you review the activities, keep in mind that some are student-directed while others are leader-directed. Also some activities may be too simplistic or too difficult for your students. Use those activities you feel are appropriate. Add your own ideas to the list. Feel free to adapt activities to meet the ages or abilities of your children. Use your imagination to make learning a fun, exciting experience as you discover new things together. Celebration centers should *involve, interest,* and *inspire.* Celebration centers should be *faith community* celebrations.

In addition to choosing the activities, you will need to gather the necessary materials to complete the activities. Some general items are needed for all the centers. These would include basic writing or craft supplies such as ruled paper, pencils, marking pens, construction paper, glue, tape, crayons, etc. You may need to provide items such as homemade play dough or items you normally keep in storage—such as tempera paint—to complete specific activities. Highlight which activities you want to do with your children as you read through the center. Then list the supplies you will need or the special arrangements you will need to make (for example, paint smocks, table coverings, or extra adult supervision). You may want to ask students, families, and friends to donate the items or to volunteer time to help complete the various activities.

CELEBRATE APOSTLES

SCRIPTURE TO READ:

Luke 6:12–16; Romans 1:1–6; 1 Corinthians 9:1–2, 12:27–31; Ephesians 2:19–22, 4:11–13; Hebrews 3:1

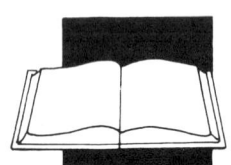

BIBLE STORIES TO LEARN:

Jesus Calls His Disciples (Mark 1:14–20); Jesus Washes the Disciples' Feet (John 13:1–20); Early Christians Spread the Good News (Acts 11:19–20); Saul Becomes a Christian (Acts 9:1–22); Paul Preaches to the Jews and Gentiles (Acts 13:44–52; 2 Timothy 1:5–12; 3:14–16)

BOOKS TO READ ABOUT APOSTLES:

Jesus' 12 Disciples (CPH, 59-1307); *Twelve Who Followed Jesus* (CPH, 59-1515); *The Coming of the Holy Spirit* (CPH, 59-1452); *Peter and the Biggest Birthday* (CPH, 59-1480)

GOD'S WORD TO REMEMBER:

Through [Jesus] and for His name's sake, we received grace and apostleship to call people from among all the Gentiles to the obedience that comes from faith. And you also are among those who are called to belong to Jesus Christ. *Romans 1:5–6*

SET UP YOUR CENTER

Place a table or desk in a corner of your classroom. In the middle of the table, put a "tent" sign that reads **Apostles Meet Here.** Also place on the table a dictionary, a Bible dictionary, a Bible, and several sample business cards. On the wall behind the table, display three sheets of poster board, each with one of these titles:

Apostles Sign In

Apostles' I.D.

Apostles' Work to Do

On a fourth sheet of poster board, write the acrostic **APOSTLE** for use in a following activity. On note cards, write the descriptions of the activities you want to use. Write a large, colorful *A* on the front of each card. Tape the cards along the edge of the table or around the posters.

ACTIVITIES

WHAT IS AN APOSTLE?

Read Luke 6:13. Look up the word *apostle* in a Bible dictionary and in a dictionary. Write your own short definition of an apostle on the **Apostles Sign In** poster.

Apostle Center

Apostle Acrostic

One poster lists the letters that spell *apostle*. Think of a word, phrase, or sentence that describes the word *apostle* and that begins with each letter in the word. Write it on the poster. Or make your own Apostle Acrostic on a sheet of construction paper.

A Specially Commissioned Person

An apostle is one sent with a special commission. Look up the word *commission* in a dictionary. Name some people you know who are commissioned or sent into special service. (Answers might include pastors, teachers, missionaries, police officers, firefighters, etc.) Write your discoveries on note cards or slips of paper and tape them to the **Apostles' Work to Do** poster.

I'm Jesus' Helper

To the teacher: Children will enjoy using a professional button maker for this activity if your school or congregation owns one.

Make a personal badge to wear so people can identify you as one of Jesus' helpers. Use marking pens to design your badge on a circle of colorful poster board or construction paper. Use masking tape to attach a large safety pin to the back of the badge. When you aren't wearing your badge, pin it to the **Apostles' I.D.** poster or hang it from a ribbon secured to the table.

Jesus' Apostles Bulletin Board or Banners

Make a bulletin board that shows Jesus' apostles. Use either faces or their symbols. Use marking pens to make nameplates for His helpers. Or make a banner for each apostle. Use felt or construction paper. Show the apostle and his symbol. Cut out letters for his name. Hang the apostolic banners in your church or fellowship hall as a reminder of Jesus' first commissioned helpers.

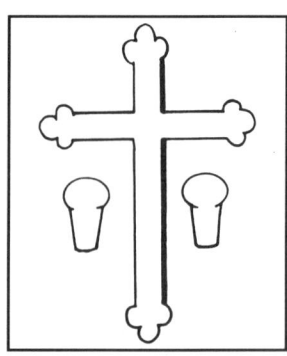
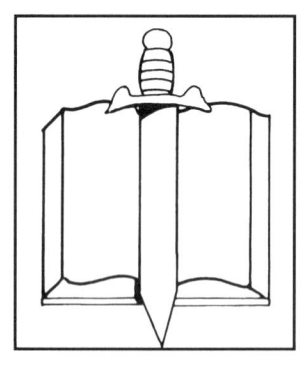

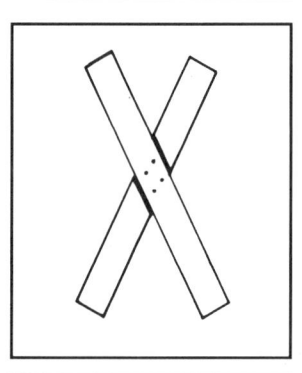
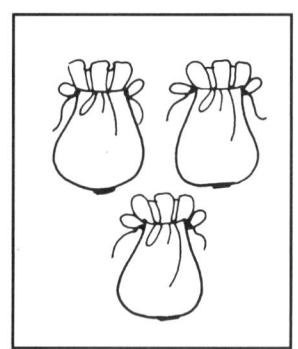
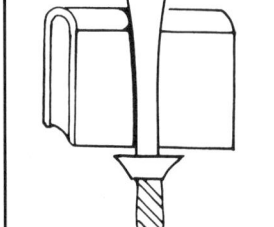

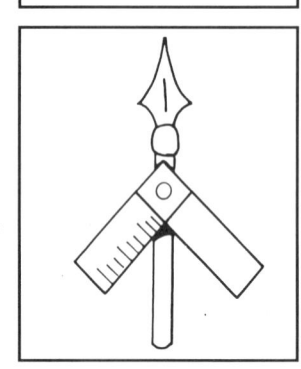

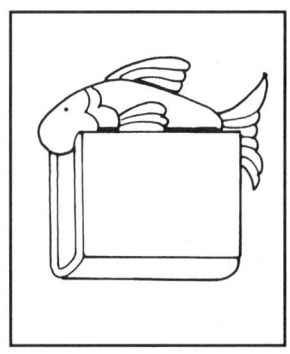

Personal Calling Cards

Look at the business cards displayed on the table. What information is on each card? A century ago, people printed calling cards to leave at a home or business after a visit. Today, business people use cards to give their name and phone number to a client or business associate. Make a calling card for yourself. What words would you write on it to show that Jesus commissions you to be His helper? What symbol would you draw to show your special service?

Apostle Pennant

Use marking pens and construction paper to design an apostle pennant for your bedroom. Write your name and some opportunites God has given to you to help others.

More Apostle Projects

- Volunteer at a community food bank. Keep a journal of your experiences and share with your class how you felt about helping others.
- Read about Jesus' apostles in the Scripture references. Write a report about one apostle and the special gift he used to help others. Thank God for the apostles He sent to help Jesus.
- Interview a Christian teacher, school principal, or missionary. Make a video that tells how God has helped that person serve Him in a special way. Report to your class what you discover.

Celebrate Baptism

Scripture to Read:

Romans 6:3–4; Ephesians 4:5; Galatians 3:26-27; Ephesians 4:4-6; 1 Peter 3:18–22

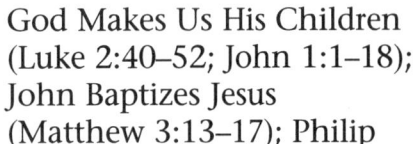

Bible Stories to Learn:

God Makes Us His Children (Luke 2:40–52; John 1:1–18); John Baptizes Jesus (Matthew 3:13–17); Philip Explains the Gospel to the Ethiopian (Acts 8:26–40); Paul Baptizes the Jailer and His Family (Acts 16:16–34)

Books to Read about Baptism:

Somebody Lives Inside (CPH, 56–1557); *The Story of Jesus' Baptism and Temptation* (CPH, 59–1503)

God's Word to Remember:

He who believes and is baptized will be saved. *Mark 16:16*

Set Up Your Center

Caption a bulletin board or a section of wall **God's Family**. Near the bulletin board, place a container with the materials for the activities you have selected.

Around the edge of the bulletin board, attach large construction paper shells with the directions for one of the activities you've selected written on each shell.

Activities

God's Family

When we are baptized, God works through the water and His Word to forgive us and make us new people through the sacrifice of His Son. Draw a large tree on a sheet of construction paper. Title it **God's Family**. Write your name on one of the tree branches. Write Jesus' name on the tree trunk. Then write names of Christians on the leaves. Don't forget your family members and Christian friends. Did you remember your pastor(s) and teacher(s)? Attach the drawing to the bulletin board.

Baptism center

Who Are My Sponsors?

When you were baptized into God's family, you probably had people serve as your sponsors or godparents. Your sponsors answered the pastor's questions for you. They said for you, "Yes, I believe in God the Father, God the Son, and God the Holy Spirit." They also promised to help you to fight Satan and be faithful to your Lord, hearing His Word and living as His child.

Find out who your sponsors or godparents are. Ask your parents more about your Baptism day. Write a thank-you note to your parents and your sponsors or godparents for bringing you to be baptized into God's family.

Thank You

Special Baptism Language

Look up the following words in a dictionary. Then write a short sentence that tells what each word means to you. Or draw and color a picture of someone being baptized and use the words to write a caption for your picture.

Baptism

Bible

cleanse

parent(s)

pastor

promise

sponsor(s)

What I Like about Baptism

Have you seen a Baptism? Describe it in your own words. Tell why the Baptism was special and what part you remember best.

I Am God's Child

Write the word *sin* on a sheet of paper. Surround it with pictures or words that describe sins you have done. When you're done, say, "I'm sorry, Lord" for each sin. Wad up the paper and throw it away. That's what God did at your Baptism. He got rid of *all* your sins. With the water and His Word, He made you clean and pure. He does that for you every day through His forgiveness. Remember your Baptism each day.

Cut a shell shape from white construction paper. Write on the shell: **God cleansed me. I am His child.** Take the shell home and tape it to your bathroom mirror. When you brush your teeth, comb your hair, or wash your face, look at your shell and remember how much God loves you.

My Second Birthday

Ask your parents the date of your baptismal birthday—the day God made you His child. That day is your "second birthday." Light a candle on your baptismal birthday. Or make a paper candle and write your baptismal birthday on it. Tape it to your bedroom wall as a reminder of that special day. Sing the following words to the tune of "The Farmer in the Dell."

The Spirit lives in me.
The Spirit lives in me.
God has made me His dear child.
The Spirit lives in me.

Baptism with Water and God's Word

To the teacher: Set up a water center. Place a vinyl tablecloth on a table or desk and pour water into a large, shallow pan.

Use your hand or a seashell to scoop up the water and let it drip into the pan. Think about the words the pastor said when you were baptized: "I baptize you in the name of the Father, and of the Son, and of the Holy Spirit. Amen."

A Special Baptismal Remembrance

On the inside of a favorite seashell, use a permanent marking pen to write your name and baptismal birthday. Outline the shell with a gold or silver glitter pen. Ask an adult to use an electric drill to make a hole in the top of the shell. Thread a silver or gold cord through the hole and tie a knot in it. Hang your baptismal remembrance in a special place or wear it around your neck.

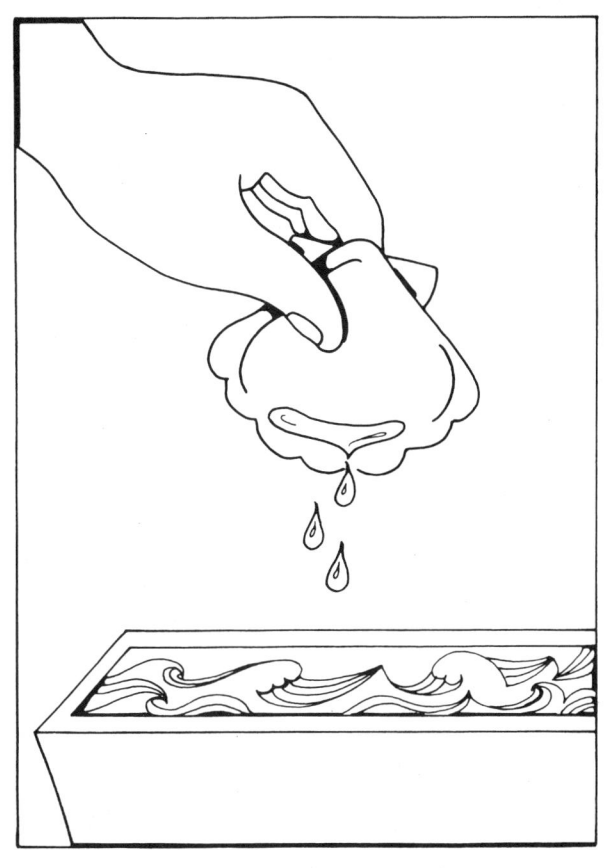

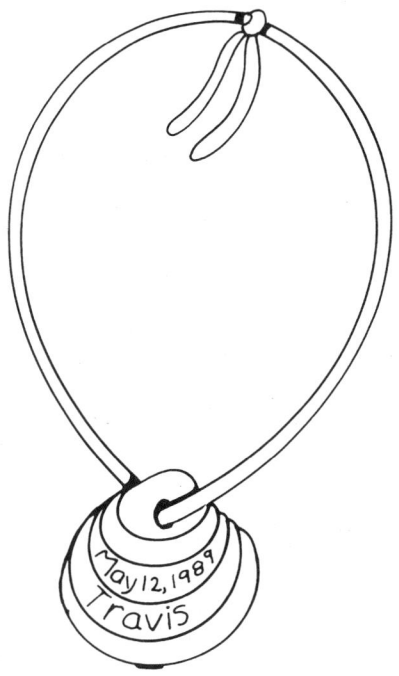

Who Baptized Whom?

(See note below.) Read Bible stories about people who were baptized. Make a chart on construction paper or poster board titled **Who Baptized Whom?** Draw a vertical line to divide the paper into two columns. Title the left-hand column **Baptizer.** Write the person's name who did the baptizing in this column. Title the right-hand column **Baptized.** Write the person's name who was baptized in this column. (For example, Philip was the baptizer, and the Ethiopian official was baptized.) Add your pastor's name and the names of your family members and friends, too.

In the Bible God worked through people who baptized others. Today God works through pastors who baptize His children.

Celebrate Creation

Scripture to Read:
Genesis 1–2

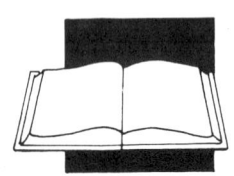

Bible Stories to Learn:
God Makes the World (Genesis 1:1–2:3); God Made and Loves People (Genesis 1:26–2:25)

Books to Read about Creation:
The Story of Creation (Concordia 56–1496); *The World God Made* (CPH, 59–1114); *God's Good Creation* (CPH, 59–1463)

God's Word to Remember:
In the beginning God created the heavens and the earth. *Genesis 1:1*

Set Up Your Center

Set a small table or desk in a corner. Hang an inflatable globe from the ceiling above the table. Place the following items on or around the table: a globe, a Bible, and the necessary materials to complete the activities you select.

Tape several full-size paper cutouts of children on the wall behind the table. On individual note cards, write the activities you selected. Place the appropriate cards inside a colorful file folder labeled with the activity title. Put the folders into a box or storage unit by the table.

Activities

Heavenly Days! Heavenly Nights!

Card 1: Read Genesis 1:1–5.
Card 2: Glue a sheet of 8" × 10" black construction paper to a piece of 11" × 17" white construction paper to represent night and day. Write a thank-You prayer to God for making both night and day.
Card 3: Keep a journal of everything you do during the daylight and everything you do during the darkness. Share it with your class. Thank God for the daylight and darkness.

Big Sky

Card 1: Read Genesis 1:6–8.
Card 2: Lie on your back outside. Watch the sky. What cloud shapes do you see? Watch the clouds move and change as the wind blows. Research *clouds* in a science book or an encyclopedia. How many kinds of clouds did you find? What are their names and characteristics?
Card 3: Draw a cloud shape or cut one from construction paper. Make more

CREATION CENTER

clouds by pulling apart cotton balls or cotton batting and gluing them to the construction paper.

Card 4: Record the types of clouds you see in the sky for one month.

Card 5: Use an instant-print camera to photograph the sky under different conditions: a bright sky, a cloudy sky, a stormy sky, a cloudless sky. Make a poster or a bulletin board display that shows God's sky.

Card 6: Write a haiku about God's sky. A haiku is a Japanese poem written in five lines. The first line is a one-syllable word. The second line has three syllables. The third and fourth lines each have five syllables. The last line ends the poem with one syllable. Sometimes a haiku ends with the same word that starts it.

Land and Sea

Card 1: Read Genesis 1:9–13.

Card 2: Make a land and sea diorama. Fill a large, shallow pan with sand or soil. Fill a small plastic container with water and place it in the sand. Add plastic greenery such as bushes, trees, and small flowers.

Card 3: God filled the deserts He created with different colors of sand. Make a desert in a jar. Make colored dust by rubbing colored chalk on a rough surface. Stir each color into a separate container of fine sand or salt. Roll and staple heavy paper to make a funnel. Pour layers of different colors of sand through the funnel into a clean glass jar. Fill the jar completely. Use a pencil to poke holes near the side of the jar to shift the sand layers and make designs. Put a tight-fitting lid on the jar. Remember not to shake it or turn the jar upside down.

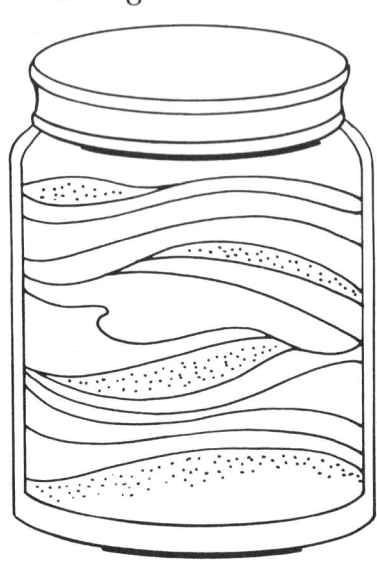

Earth and All Stars

Card 1: Read Genesis 1:14–19.

Card 2: Cover half of a sheet of white construction paper with black construction paper. Attach star stickers to the night side. Use a silver or white crayon to draw the moon. Add silver glitter to the moon. Color a bright sun on the day side. Add gold glitter to the sun.

Card 3: Look up *sun, moon,* and *stars* in an encyclopedia or science book. Why is the sun such an important heavenly body for our earth? Learn the names of the constellations and look for them in a clear, night sky.

Card 4: Sing "Earth and All Stars" or "Jesus in the Morning." Thank God for the sun, moon, and stars.

Card 5: God made the lights in the sky, but the best light He gave to the world is Jesus. Read about Jesus, the Light of the world, in John 1:1–9; 8:12; 12:46. Use a glitter pen to write **Jesus Is My Light** on a fat white candle. Take the candle home and light it during family devotions.

Card 6: List the lights in your life on a sheet of paper. Your list might include a flashlight, a reading light, and a dusk-to-dawn light. It also might include people who have inspired you in specific ways. Thank God for His many lights for your life—especially for Jesus, the strongest, brightest, and saving Light.

Card 7: Cover a cardboard star with aluminum foil. Tape a colorful crepe paper streamer to each of the star's points. Have a praise parade as everyone sings "Praise Him, Praise Him" or "Earth and All Stars."

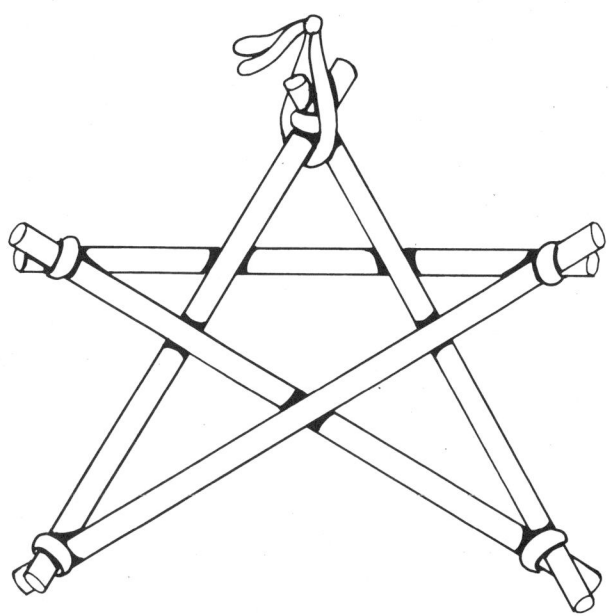

Card 8: Tape drinking straws together to form five-pointed stars. Cut yarn or cord to make hangers for the stars. Attach them to the ceiling or to a clothesline stretched across a corner of the room.

SWIMMERS AND FLYERS

To the teacher: Bring a pet bird in a cage to the classroom. Set up a small tropical fish aquarium. Gather resource books about animals, birds, and insects and place these on a reading table. Have children help feed and care for the animals.

Card 1: Read Genesis 1:20–23.

Card 2: Keep a journal that describes what the bird does during the day, what it eats, and what it needs to stay alive. Do the same with the fish. How has God made each fish and bird unique? Which are your favorites and why?

Card 3: Start a collection of flying insects. Identify each by its common and scientific names. How does each insect help our world?

Card 4: Cut pictures of water creatures, birds, and flying insects from magazines. Label separate sheets of poster board or construction paper as **Water Creatures**, **Birds**, and **Flying Insects**. Glue each picture to the appropriate poster. Thank God for each individual creature.

GOD'S AMAZING ANIMALS

Card 1: Read Genesis 1:24–25.

Card 2: Cut pictures of animals and people from magazines. Label separate sheets of poster board or construction paper as **Livestock, Wild Animals, Pets,** and **Humans.** Glue each picture to the appropriate poster. Thank God for each individual creature.

Card 3: Make an **Alphabet Animals** wall. Find a picture or draw an animal for each letter of the alphabet in sequence.

Card 4: Make recycled wrapping paper for gift giving. Cut apart brown paper grocery bags and place them flat on a table. Cut a potato or an apple in half and carve an animal shape or animal footprint into the fleshy portion. Dip the carved side into tempera paint, then repeatedly press it onto the paper to make prints. Let dry.

To the teacher: Follow the recipe to make newspaper mash to complete the following activity.

NEWSPAPER MASH RECIPE:

Tear newspaper into 1" square pieces. Soak overnight in twice as much water as newspaper. Drain and squeeze out excess water. Put paper pulp into bowl. Add enough flour paste to hold pulp together. Knead until workable.

Add flour if too wet. (For *instant* flour paste, stir ½ cup flour and ½ cup water together in a bowl. Paste should look thick and creamy. Add flour or water if necessary. Refrigerate in a tightly covered container. For *cooked* flour paste, combine ½ cup flour, 2 tablespoons sugar, and 2 cups water together in a pan. Heat and stir until mixture boils. Keep stirring until paste thickens. Refrigerate as above.)

Card 5: Make creation pencil toppers. Mold a glob of newspaper mash into a simple head shape. When the shape is close to the form you want, insert a pencil into the neck. Remold the head to fit onto the pencil. Stick the pencil into the bottom of an upside-down egg carton to dry. Use marking pens to decorate the topper. Dip the marking pen in water so the color will flow better over the rough surface.

AMAZING ME

Card 1: Read Genesis 1:26–31.

Card 2: Place newsprint or butcher paper on the floor. Ask a friend to trace your body with a pencil as you lie on the paper. Cut out your body and tape it on a wall. Color your body shape to look like you. Add the names of the parts of your body on the paper person: head, arms, hands, chest, stomach, legs, feet. As you write each body part, say, "Thank You, God, for making my (*head*)."

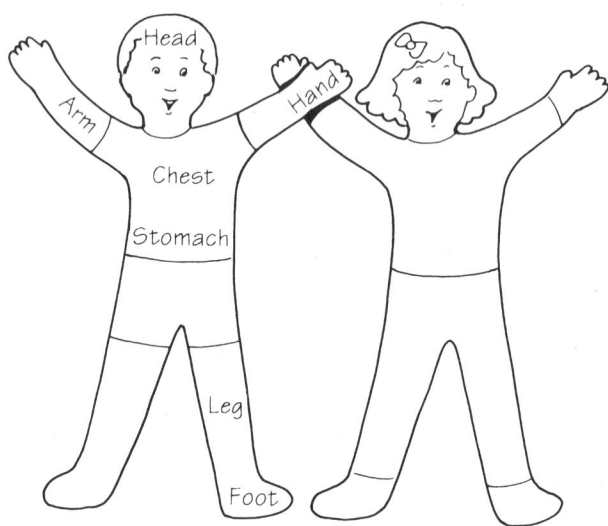

Card 3: Cut a snowflake from white construction paper. Write your name on the snowflake. Think about your unique beauty. Ask several classmates to make snowflakes. Pass the snowflakes around and write statements on the snowflakes such as "Trevor is patient." "Kathy always listens." "Rob always takes time to play catch." Thank God for each of your friends and their unique gifts.

Card 4: God has made us caretakers of His beautiful earth. List your favorite places on earth on a sheet of paper. Then describe how you can help take care of these places.

Card 5: Become involved in activities that care for the earth.

Card 6: Start a rainbow garden. Decorate Styrofoam cups with marking pens, then fill them with potting soil. Plant one or two bean seeds; a few marigold seeds; or a cutting from a plant such as coleus, Swedish ivy, or philodendron. Place the cups on a tray where they will get natural daylight. Water the plants when the soil feels dry.

To the teacher: To prepare for the following activity, make a sculpture block for each child or duplicate the directions so children can complete the project at home.

Plaster Recipe:

Mix equal parts plaster of paris and vermiculite (available at garden shops). Add enough water to make a thick, cream-like paste.
Pour the mixture into a half-gallon or gallon jug. Let harden completely.

Card 7: Make a creation carving. Carefully peel away the carton from the plaster. Use a table knife or a spoon to carve the block (a sharp knife is not needed). Make an animal or a person.

Card 8: Make a creation collage. Cut pictures of plants, animals, and people from magazines. Glue them to a paper plate. Punch holes around the outside edge of the plate, about ½" from the edge and about 1" apart. Lace yarn or cord in and out of the holes, then tie a loop at the top. Hang the creation collage where it will remind you of God's creation.

Celebrate Death and Resurrection

Scripture to Read:

Psalm 23:4; Matthew 28:7; John 11:25–26; Romans 4:25; Revelation 14:13

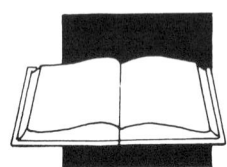

Bible Stories to Learn:

Jesus Raises Jairus' Daughter (Luke 8:40–56); Jesus Raises Lazarus (John 11:1–44); Jesus Dies for All People (Luke 22:26–56; John 29:28–42); Jesus Rises from the Dead (Luke 24:1–11; John 20:1–18); Jesus' Power over Death (1 Corinthians 15:20–23)

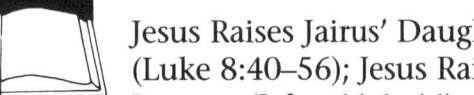

Books to Read about Death and Resurrection:

If I Should Die, If I Should Live (CPH, 56–1317); *What Happened When Grandma Died?* (CPH, 56–1458); *Balloons for Trevor* (CPH, 56–1516); *Jesus and Jairus' Little Girl* (CPH, 56–1479); *The Day Jesus Died* (CPH, 56–1516); *Good Friday* (CPH, 59–1451); *My Happy Easter Book* (CPH, 56–1493); *The Easter Women* (CPH, 59–1431); *God's Easter Plan* (CPH, 56–1461); *Jesus Is Alive* (CPH, 56–1626); *The Story of the Empty Tomb* (CPH, 59–1517)

God's Word to Remember:

Because I live, you also will live. *John 14:19*

He is not here; He has risen! *Luke 24:6*

Set Up Your Center

In a corner of your room, decorate for Easter with colorful crepe paper; Easter vinyl clings; a faith-related wall hanging; "new life" items such as plants and flowers; pictures of baby animals; and a poster of the risen Jesus. Place baskets filled with Easter grass and large plastic eggs, each containing a note card with the directions for a selected activity. Place items necessary to complete the selected activities in a storage container.

Activities

Make a Connection

What do you know about death from your family experiences? Have you been to a funeral or watched a burial? List what your parents, relatives, or friends have told you about death. Study one of the stories of Jesus conquering death. On another sheet of paper, write the following:

Jesus gave His life for me on the cross. But He rose again on Easter morning. Because He lives, I will live with Him forever.

Throw away the sheet of paper with your questions, fears, and old experiences of death. Tape the paper with the joyful message where you will be reminded of Jesus' promise of eternal life.

DEATH AND RESSURECTION CENTER

WATCH THE CATERPILLAR

Place a caterpillar in a large, clean mayonnaise jar. Add a few green leaves and a couple of twigs. Use a hammer and a nail to make holes in the lid. Place the lid on the jar and set it in a cool, dry place where you can watch the caterpillar every day. How many days did it take for the caterpillar to make its cocoon or chrysalis? List ways that the caterpillar appears to be dead. Look up *caterpillar* and *chrysalis* in a science book or an encyclopedia. What kind of butterfly or moth will your caterpillar become? Thank God for the new life He gives!

THANK GOD FOR NEW LIFE

- Plant fast-growing seeds such as beans or marigolds in Styrofoam cups. Place the cups in a sunny window. When the plants develop a root system, transplant them into a small outdoor garden, if weather and space permits. Or transplant them to a larger container. Thank Jesus for the new life He gives you.
- Plant an amaryllis bulb in a container of potting soil. Place the pot in a sunny window. Water it when the soil feels dry. Watch the green leaves and stem grow rapidly. You may have to tie the stalk to a ruler or dowel rod as it grows. Watch your amaryllis bloom.
- Cover the bottom of a shallow container or cake pan with a layer of gravel. Lay narcissus, crocus, or hyacinth bulbs point upward on top of the gravel. Add enough water so the water just touches the bulbs. Check the water level every day. "Force" the bulbs to bloom by placing the container in a sunny window. Watch the leaves and stems grow. In four to six weeks, you should see buds and blooms.

BUTTERFLY SOAP

Paint simple butterfly shapes on bars of soap using paintbrushes and tempera paints. Or use table knives to carve butterfly shapes from bars of bath soap. The butterfly reminds us of new life. Christians use the butterfly as a symbol for Easter and the resurrection.

BUTTERFLY PRINTS

Purchase pre-cut butterfly soap shapes from a bath shop. Pour thick tempera paint into shallow plastic tubs. Dip the butterfly shape lightly into the paint, then press it onto a paper bag, plain wrapping paper, or construction paper. Make each print lighter than the previous one. Allow the printed paper to dry thoroughly, then use it for wrapping gifts or to make note cards.

NEW LIFE ACROSTIC

Write the letters for **New Life** down the left side of a sheet of construction paper. Then think of a word or phrase that describes God's gift of new life through Jesus and that begins with each letter. You might make your acrostic into a prayer or a free-verse poem.

Never have to fear death.
Eternal life with Jesus.
Way cool!

Living out my love for Jesus.
In my Father's house.
Freedom from sin and death.
Everlasting praises.

CELEBRATE EASTER

SCRIPTURE TO READ:

John 11:25; Romans 6:5; Revelation 20:6

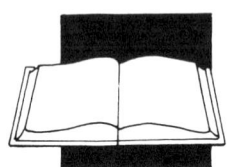

BIBLE STORIES TO LEARN:

Jesus Rises from the Dead (Mark 16:1–8; Luke 24:1–12; John 20:1–18); Jesus Shows His Power over Death (1 Corinthians 15:20–23)

BOOKS TO READ ABOUT EASTER:

Jesus Is Alive (CPH, 56–1626); *My Happy Easter Book* (CPH, 56–1493); *The Easter Women* (CPH, 59–1431); *God's Easter Plan* (CPH, 56–1461); *Thomas, the Doubting Disciple* (CPH, 59–1504); *The Story of the Empty Tomb* (CPH, 59–1517)

GOD'S WORD TO REMEMBER:

Just as Christ was raised from the dead through the glory of the Father, we too may live a new life. *Romans 6:4*

SET UP YOUR CENTER

Set up a large wooden cross and drape a white cloth around the "arms." You might add silk Easter lilies to the cross or place potted lilies at the foot of the cross.

Collect boxes of various sizes. In each box, place the directions and supplies for one of the activities you selected. On the top of each box, glue a white cross. Use a marking pen to write **Jesus is alive!** on each cross.

ACTIVITIES

THE CROSS IS EMPTY! JESUS IS ALIVE!

Use twigs or small sticks of approximately the same diameter to make a cross. A stick about 5" or 6" long works best. Use leather lacing, jute, or twine to lash the twigs together. Use craft glue to attach a silk flower or sprig of dried flowers to the center of the cross. Display the cross at home as a reminder of God's awesome love and forgiveness for you through Jesus.

24

Easter center

Kids of the King

Early Christians often decorated their churches with peacock feathers. The peacock—the king of all birds—was a symbol of the resurrection. When the peacock sheds its feathers in late summer, this symbolizes the death of our earthly bodies. Soon after Christmas, the peacock regrows its royal-looking plumage. This represents the glorified, perfect, beautiful body that God will give to each Christian at the resurrection. (Read more about the peacock in an encyclopedia or animal book.) Because of Jesus' death and resurrection, kids of the King look forward to living with Him in a perfect heavenly home.

Make a colorful peacock feather-fan from construction paper. Wear it as a reminder that Jesus is your King and that He gives you life in His royal family of believers.

Resurrection Sun Cross

To the teacher: Duplicate the cross pattern on page 58, one for each child. Enlarge or reduce the pattern as needed.

On Good Friday, Jesus was nailed to the cross to suffer and die for the sins of all people. That is good news on what must have been a sad day for Jesus' friends. But the *best* news is that Jesus is *alive!* He kept His promise. He followed God's plan and took our place on the cross. He poured out His blood for our sins. His body and blood—shed for us—gives us the forgiveness we need each day. Jesus gives us joy, hope, and sunshine for every day of our lives as we live in His love.

Tape the pattern of the cross and sun to a thick board. Ask an adult to help you hammer small nails through the markings, trying to keep the nails about ½" above the board. Carefully tear away the paper and throw it away.

Wind embroidery floss or string around the outline of the cross three or four times. Choose another color to wind around the circle of the sun. As you tie a knot to begin or end a particular color of string or floss, dot the knot with glue to secure it.

Attach a picture holder to the back of the board. Hang your sun cross at home as a reminder that Jesus died and rose again for you.

Storytelling Together

Use play dough or clay to make a cave-like tomb. Roll a large ball of play dough or clay to make the stone that covered the entrance. Stick small, leafy twigs into lumps of clay for the trees and bushes around the tomb. Use plastic people to represent the angel, Mary, and Jesus. Read the Easter story in the Bible. Take turns using the props to act out the story. Use your own words to tell the story. Remind one another how wonderful it is that Jesus died and rose again.

Grace Notes

Wave scarves or ribbons and dance as you sing the following words to the tune of "The Farmer in the Dell." Write your own stanzas too!

Our Jesus is alive!
Our Jesus is alive!
He's no longer on the cross.
Our Jesus is alive!

He rose for you and me!
He rose for you and me!
Sing, dance, and shout "Hooray!"
He rose for you and me!

Easter People

Cut a large cross from construction paper. Write your name vertically down the left side on one side of the cross. Turn it over and write **Jesus** vertically down the left side. Ask friends to write one good thing about you that begins with each letter in your name. Turn the cross over and write one good thing about Jesus that begins with each letter in His name. Punch a hole in the top of the cross. Cut a length of yarn or string and tie it through the hole as a hanger. Display the cross as a reminder to thank Jesus every day for His love and for your friends.

Paper Egg People Messengers

To the teacher: Duplicate the pattern on page 59, several copies for each child. Enlarge or reduce as needed.

Let's share the good news of Jesus' resurrection with others through our words and through the objects we give away.

Use crayons or marking pens to color the egg people. Cut them out. Overlap the ends around the back and tape or staple them. Place a hard-boiled egg inside the egg person. Fold the sleeves toward the front. On a slip of paper, write a message or a favorite Bible verse that tells the Good News that Jesus is alive. Here are some things you could say:

Jesus died for you.
Jesus loves you!
God loved the world and sent Jesus to save us!—John 3:16
God is love.
Happy Easter! Jesus is alive!

Punch a hole in each end of the paper. Thread yarn or string through the holes and tie the ends together. Hang the Good News message on your paper egg person. Give your Easter messenger to someone who needs to hear the Good News about Jesus.

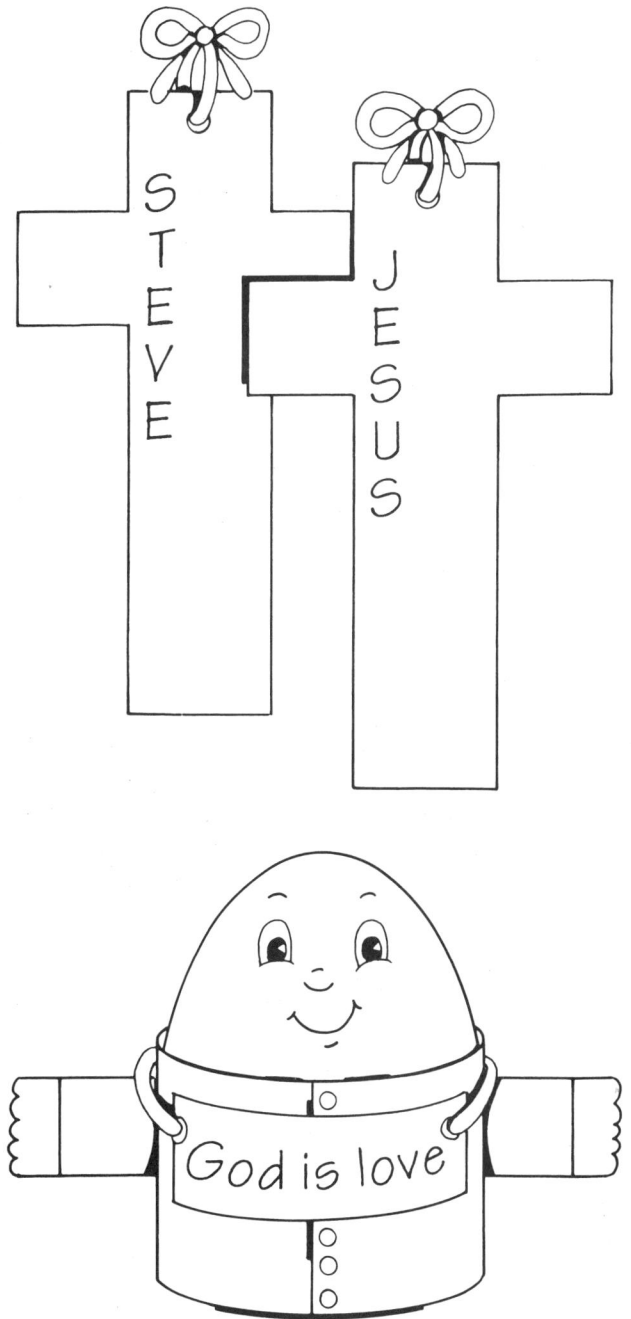

Easter Egg Surprises

Have an Easter egg scavenger hunt. Cut 10 slips of paper so each will fit inside a plastic Easter egg. Number the slips 1 through 10. Write a Bible verse on each slip of paper and a clue about where to find the next egg. When the last egg is found, provide a special surprise for each child.

Celebrate Forgiveness

Scripture to Read:

Colossians 3:13

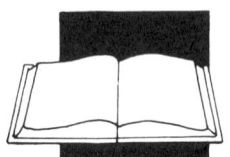

Bible Stories to Learn:

God Rescues Adam and Eve (Genesis 3:1–24); God Helps Joseph Forgive His Brothers (Genesis 42:1–45:15; 50:15–21); Nicodemus Visits Jesus (John 3:1–21); Jesus Talks with a Samaritan Woman (John 4:1–42); Jesus Helps Us Love and Forgive One Another (Matthew 18:21–35); Jesus Gives Us the Lord's Supper (Luke 22:7–20); Jesus Forgives Others (Luke 23:32–34, 39–43)

Books to Read about Forgiveness:

The Fall into Sin (CPH, 56–1486); *Joseph Forgives His Brothers* (CPH, 56–1494); *The Father Who Forgave* (CPH, 56–1275); *The Prodigal Son* (CPH, 59–1495); *The Bread and the Wine* (CPH, 59–1245); *The Very First Lord's Supper* (CPH, 59–1501); *Jesus Forgives Peter* (CPH, 59–1293)

God's Word to Remember:

Be kind and compassionate to one another, forgiving each other, just as in Christ God forgave you. *Ephesians 4:32*

Set Up Your Center

Trace the outline of a person onto a sheet of butcher paper. Cut out the paper person. Add a bright red heart and a happy face. Attach the person to a wall and tape the arms around a clean trash container. Add a speech bubble near the paper person that reads **I forgive**. Place directions for the activities you have selected and the necessary supplies into paper bags of various sizes. Draw a red heart on each bag.

Activities

Read and Learn about Forgiveness

Work with a group of three or four to complete this activity. Write words that make you think about forgiveness on slips of paper. You might write *forgive, forgiven, forgiveness, acceptance, sin, love, grace, mercy,* and *forget*. Put the slips of paper in a cup. Pass the cup around the group and ask each person to take out one slip. Take turns telling about a situation that relates to the word. Then work together to use Bibles and concordances to find Bible verses about each word. Make a poster that shows your words and the Bible references about those words that you found.

FORGIVENESS CENTER

MAKE A FORGIVENESS BOX

Cover an empty tissue box or cereal box with construction paper. Write **Medicine for the Soul** on the box. Add a colorful heart or attach heart stickers. Then cut strips of paper long enough to write on. On each strip of paper, write a phrase that would make someone feel better after they have done something wrong. Use phrases such as

Jesus forgives me. I forgive you.
Jesus loves you and made you God's child.
Jesus died and lives for you!
God is our helper.
God is love.
I love you because …

When you want to ask for forgiveness or when you want to forgive another person, take a strip of paper from the box, read it together, and give each other a hug.

BLESS ONE ANOTHER

Ask a friend to pray with you. Take turns saying sentence prayers. Then bless each other as you make the sign of the cross just like your pastor does in church. In this way you are reminded of your Baptism. Give each other a blessing such as

God bless and keep you.

Jesus loves and forgives you.

I love and forgive you too.

God makes us part of His family.

I thank God for you.

PLAY "REFLECTIONS"

Use a pizza circle as the base to make a game spinner. Use a marking pen to divide the circle into eight sections. Make a hole in the center and use a paper fastener to attach a spinner cut from poster board. Make sure the spinner can move freely. On each section of the circle, print one of the following:

- Tell about something you did that makes you feel ashamed or embarrassed.
- What have you done at school that's gotten you in trouble?
- Tell about a time when a friend said or did something that hurt you.
- Tell how you felt when you asked someone to forgive you.
- What can friends do to help each other?
- Describe what happened when someone asked you to forgive him or her.
- What is one special memory you have of being in church or Sunday school?
- What are three important qualities you think people need for success?

Take turns spinning and answering the question or providing the information. If someone doesn't want to answer, pass the spinner to the next person.

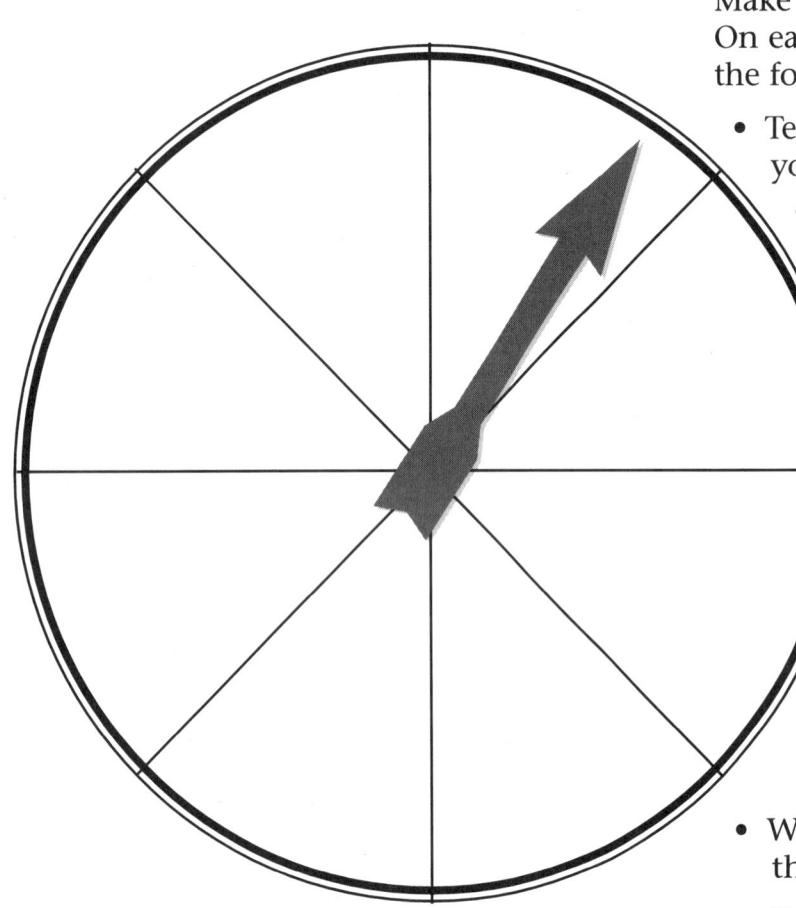

MAKE A FORGIVENESS BOOK

Cut pictures of people's faces from magazines. Look for people who are happy, angry, scared, excited, sad, eager, etc. Glue the pictures to the pages of a small notebook. Or insert the pictures into the sleeves of a small photo album.

Write short stories about each person in the book. Tell what might have happened to make the person feel the way he or she appears in the picture. What could be done to make the sad or scared people happy? Remember to write about the love and forgiveness that Jesus gives us each day. He doesn't like the bad things we do, but He loves us and died to win us forgiveness for our sins.

CIRCLE OF TRUE FRIENDS WEB

Title a sheet of construction paper **Circle of True Friends**. Draw a circle in the middle of the paper. Write Jesus' name inside the circle. Add more circles around the center circle. Write your name in one circle and the names of your friends in the others. Connect the circles with lines to show who knows whom. Make sure you connect Jesus' circle to the web too! It is through His love that we can be true friends.

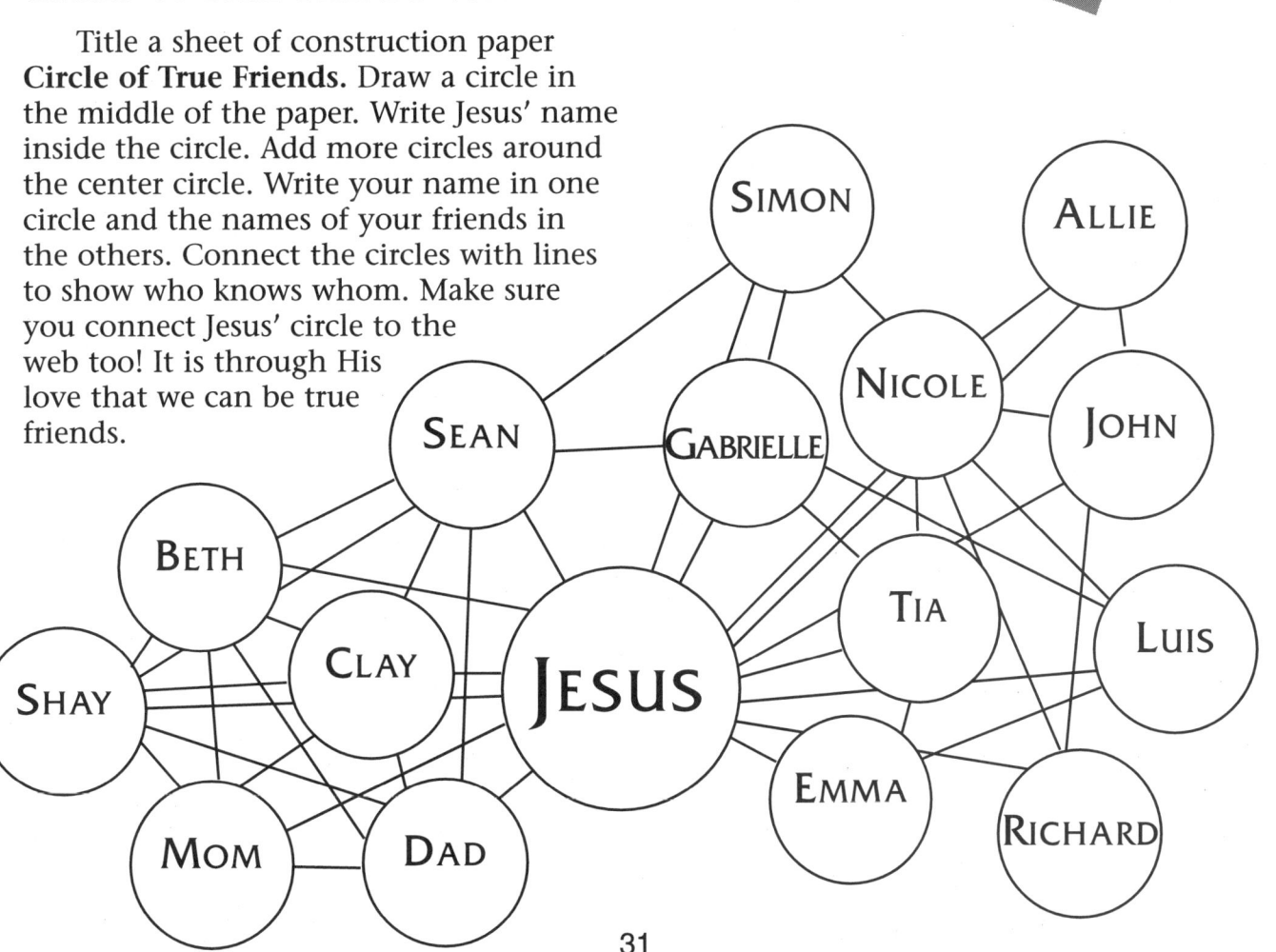

Celebrate Gospel

Scripture to Read:

Romans 1:16–17; 1 Corinthians 1:17; 15:1–4; Colossians 1:21–23

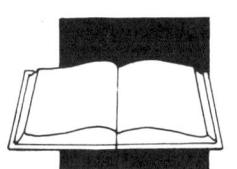

Bible Stories to Learn:

The Savior Brings Joy (Luke 1:39–55; Philippians 4:4–5); Jesus Is Born (Luke 2:1–20); Stephen Tells about Jesus (Acts 6:1–7:60); Paul Proclaims the Good News (Acts 14:8–18; 16:6–15; 17:1–34); Paul Baptizes the Jailer and His Family (Acts 16:16–34)

Books to Read about the Gospel:

Mary's Story (CPH, 59–1140); *God Promised Us a Savior* (CPH, 59–1442); *Mary's Christmas Story* (CPH, 59–1499); *Baby Jesus Is Born* (CPH, 59–1467); *My Merry Christmas Arch Book* (CPH, 59–1488); *Baby Jesus, Prince of Peace* (CPH, 59–1471)

God's Word to Remember:

For God so loved the world that He gave His one and only Son, that whoever believes in Him shall not perish but have eternal life. *John 3:16*

I am not ashamed of the Gospel, because it is the power of God for the salvation of everyone who believes. *Romans 1:16*

Set Up Your Center

Hang colorful poster board from the ceiling. On each side of the poster, print the words **Good News!** in large, decorative letters. Place gift-wrapped boxes of various sizes below the poster. On the side of each box, tape an envelope with the instructions for one of the activities you have selected. Print **Good News!** on the front of each envelope. Place the necessary supplies for each activity inside the box.

Activities

We Have Good News!

Look through the newspaper for good news stories. Cut photos and headlines that share the good news of people being rescued or healed of diseases. Glue the photos and headlines to a sheet of poster board. Title the poster **We Have Good News.** Thank God for giving these people another opportunity to live.

What Good News does God give to your family? Add drawings and headlines to the poster that tell about the good things God does for you. Some suggestions include:

Jesus saved us from sin, death, and the devil.

Jesus forgives our sins.

Jesus lives with us.

GOSPEL CENTER

God answered our prayers and made Grandma well again.

God blessed us with our new baby.

Jesus took Grandpa to heaven.

Thank God for the Good News He gives you in Jesus Christ.

PROCLAMATION PIÑATA

A proclamation is a message that someone tells someone else. For example, a mayor might tell the city that a certain day is "Plant a New Tree Day." He signs the *proclamation* stating his wishes. When a pastor tells the congregation that Jesus has forgiven their sins, it is a proclamation of the Good News.

Write proclamations and favorite Bible verses on slips of paper that tell the Good News about Jesus. Some messages might include

Jesus has been born.

Jesus died on the cross to win us forgiveness.

Jesus came back to life again.

Jesus lives with us each day.

Someday Jesus will take us to live with Him in heaven.

Make colorful decorations called piñatas. Start with a paper lunch bag. Crumple newspaper or tissue paper and stuff it inside the bag. Fill the bag two thirds full. Tie the top of the bag with string or yarn. Use construction paper, tissue paper, glue, and scissors to make the bag look like a butterfly, fish, bird, person, or flower. When the bag is decorated, carefully untie the string, remove some of the stuffing, and add small treats and your proclamations. Tie the bag shut again and hang your piñata from the ceiling.

It's a tradition in South America and Mexico to blindfold party-goers and have them strike at a piñata with a stick until it breaks open and the treats fall out. Use a plastic baseball bat instead of a stick. Or play "hot potato" by passing the piñata in a circle. At a signal, the person holding the piñata may tear a hole in the paper bag. Continue passing it around until the hole becomes large enough to dump out the treats. Read the proclamations together.

DISCOVER THE GOOD NEWS!

Make a decoder telescope. Cover one end of a paper towel tube with a 4" square of blue cellophane. Secure the cellophane with a rubber band. Decorate your decoder telescope with construction paper, tissue paper, wrapping paper, or stickers.

Use a red crayon to write a message on an index card that tells the Good News about Jesus. Your message might be "Jesus loves Megan!" or "Jesus is alive!" Color over the message with a blue crayon until you can't see the words.

Ask a friend to look through the de-coder telescope to discover the secret message. The red words should appear because the blue cellophane makes the blue crayon invisible. (If it doesn't work, add one or two more pieces of blue cellophane.)

Good News Table Screens

Japanese artists are known for making beautiful folding screens. Some of these are used as miniature tabletop decorations.

You can make a "Good News" table screen. Fold one 9" × 12" sheet of white poster board in half. Fold one side in half again toward the back center fold. Fold the other side in half toward the back center fold. It should be folded accordion style. Place the screen flat on a table. Use marking pens, crayons, and glitter pens to decorate the screen. (The Japanese often use flowers in their artwork.) Add words or short phrases that share the message "God is love" and "Jesus loves you." Add pictures of family members and friends to the screen and color decorative borders around the pictures. Remember to decorate the back of the table screen too!

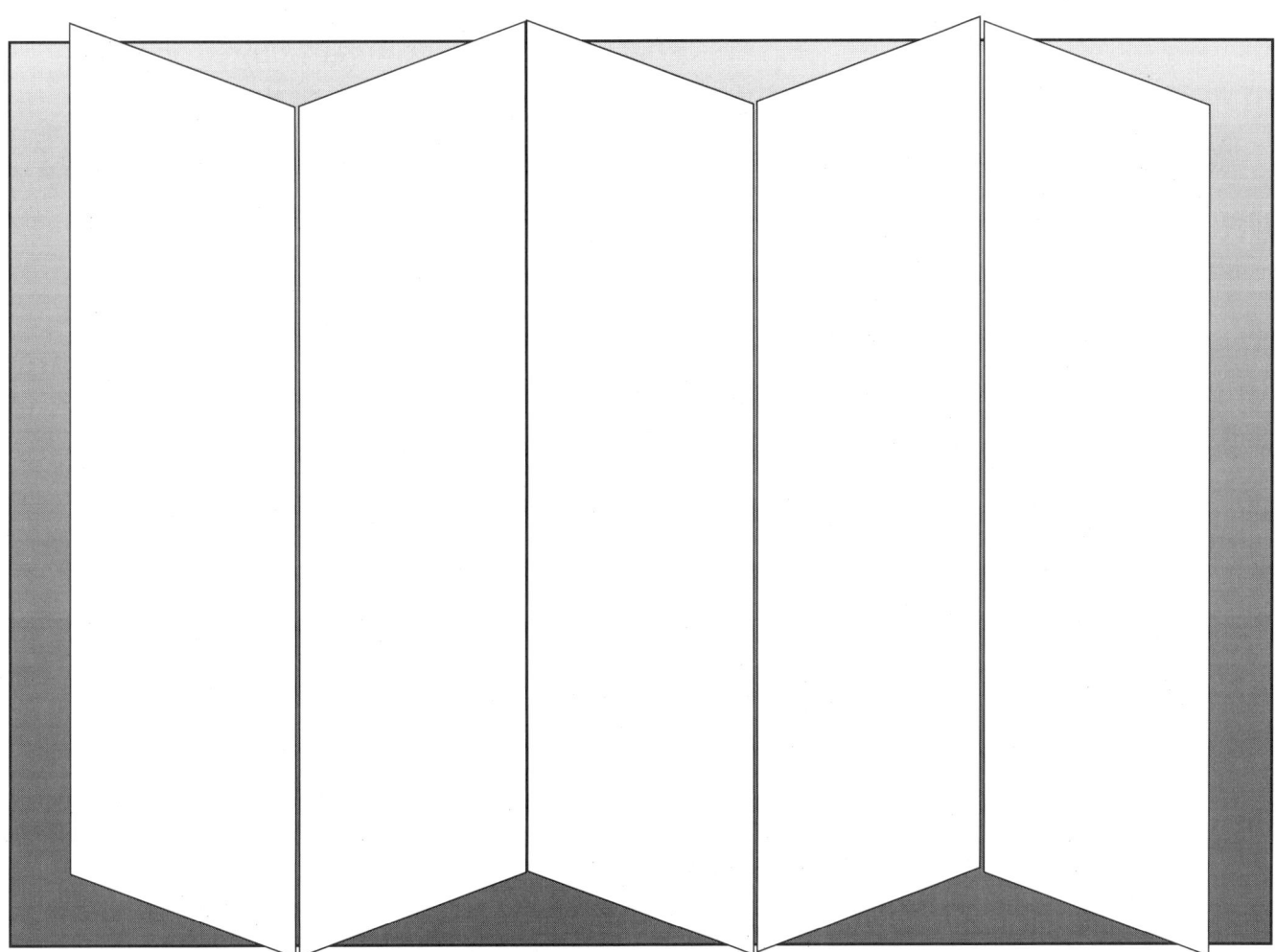

Good News Phones

To the teacher: Provide play telephones, walkie-talkies, or aluminum cans connected with string for this activity.

Find a partner and ask, "What good news have you heard lately? Let's have a conversation and fill it with only good news." Talk with each other. How many different pieces of good news can you think of to tell each other? Remember to share the best news of all—Jesus is our Savior!

Celebrate Heaven

Scripture to Read:

Genesis 1:1; Deuteronomy 26:15; Isaiah 66:1; Luke 10:20; Philippians 3:20; Revelation 19:11–16; 21:1–5

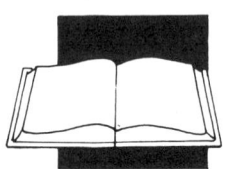

Bible Stories to Learn:

Jesus Will Take Us to Heaven (Matthew 25:31–46; 28:16–20); Jesus Ascends into Heaven (Acts 1:1–11)

Books to Read about Heaven:

Jesus Returns to Heaven (CPH, 56–1476)

God's Word to Remember:

Rejoice that your names are written in heaven. *Luke 10:20*

Set Up Your Center

Make this center area "heavenly" by draping one or more white sheets over a rope to make a tent. Or cover a card table with white sheets. Use gold and silver glitter paint to add stars and happy faces to the sheets. Spray paint cardboard boxes with gold and silver paint. Place the directions and materials for each activity you choose in a separate box. Place the boxes around the center.

Activities

What Do You Know about Heaven?

Read the Bible verses listed about heaven. Look up *heaven* in your Bible's concordance and see if you can find more passages to read. Think about heaven and write your thoughts on a sheet of paper. Draw a picture of heaven too. As you work, think about questions such as

- What do you think heaven will look like? smell like? sound like? feel like? taste like?
- Whom will you see in heaven when Jesus takes all believers there to live with Him?
- Name more people you want to be sure to see in heaven.
- How do we know we will live with Jesus in our heavenly home when we die?

Prayer Reminder

Heaven is called our eternal home (Ecclesiastes 12:5). Fold a sheet of construction paper in half. On one half, draw a picture of a house. Use gold and silver glitter pens to decorate the house. Write **Heaven is our eternal home** under the house. Write a simple prayer on the other side of the paper that thanks God for giving us the gift of heaven and life with Him forever. Take the paper home and set it in the middle of your table. Use the prayer before or after a meal or during your family devotions.

36

Heaven center

Crown of Life

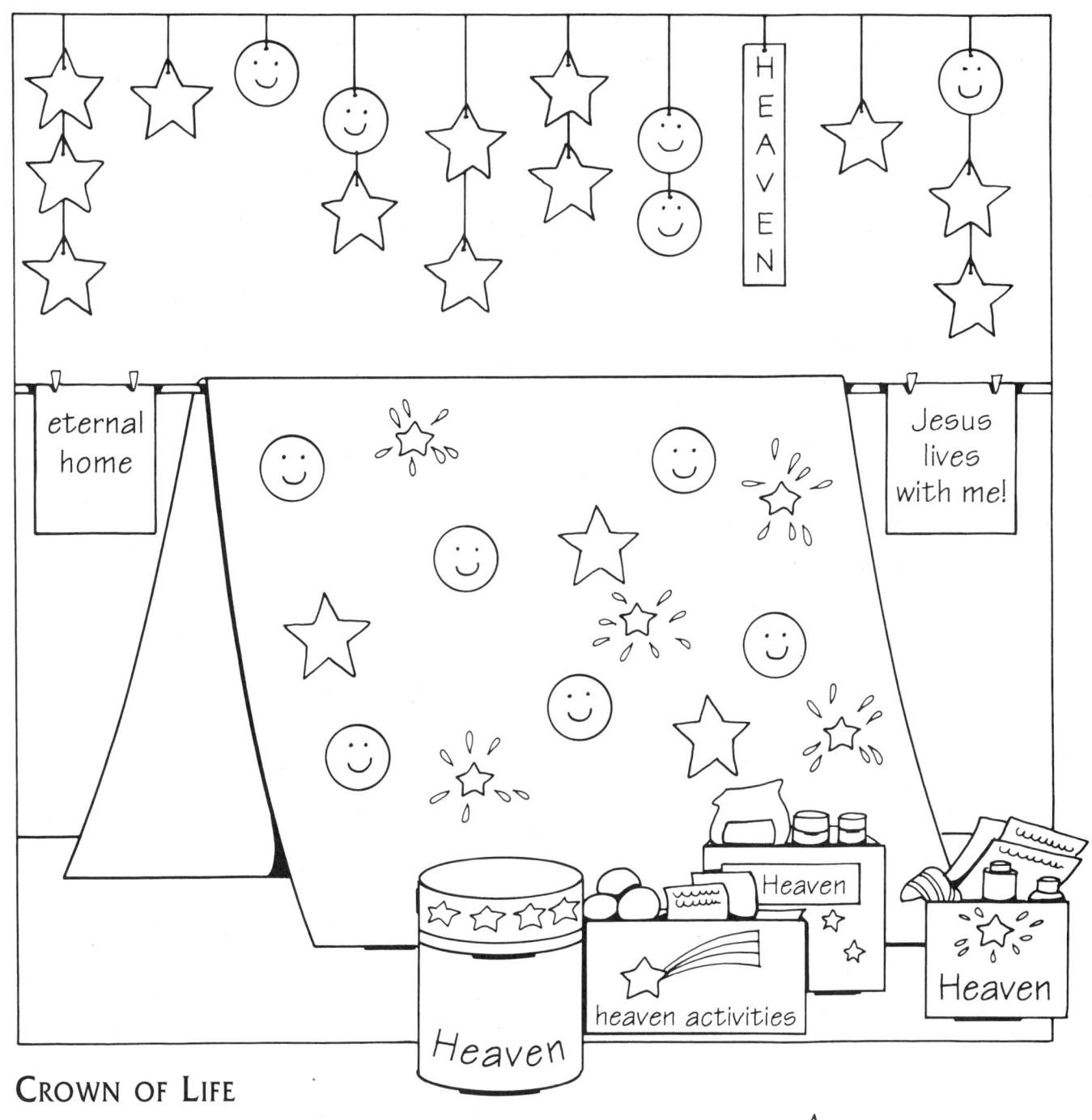

God promises those who believe in Him the crown of life—eternal life with Him in heaven. Read James 1:12 and Revelation 2:10. The crown in these passages refers to a garland or wreath given to the winner in sports contests, just like the olive wreaths the first Olympiad winners wore on their heads. Use twist ties to secure real or silk ivy into a small wreath.

37

Take it home and put it on your table. Place a votive candle inside the wreath. Light it during your meal to remind you of God's glory and grace through Jesus, the Light of our world.

Build a Heavenly Home

To the teacher: Use the following recipe to make the "glue" for building the house.

Glue Icing: Beat two egg whites and ½ teaspoon cream of tartar on high speed for one minute. Gradually add 3 cups powdered sugar and beat until the icing forms peaks. Add little or no water (1 tablespoon at a time) to thin the icing as needed. Cover the bowl with a damp cloth while you work to prevent the icing from getting hard.

Use graham crackers and icing to build a "heavenly" home. Use the icing like glue to connect graham crackers for the walls and roof. Use more icing to stick gumdrops and candies on the house. Take it home and set it on your table as a reminder of the perfect home Jesus has ready for you in heaven.

Heavenly Wear

Use fabric paint to decorate the front and back of a cotton T-shirt. Use words and pictures that tell everyone who sees your shirt that you are happy about the gift of heaven. You'll need to wash your T-shirt inside out in cold water and dry it on low heat.

Heaven Is My Home

Decorate a brightly colored visor with fabric paint and permanent marking pens. Wear it to help witness your faith to those around you. Use some of these phrases

Heaven is my home.
Jesus waits for me in heaven.
Jesus + me = heaven.
I look forward to heaven!
Heaven keeps me looking up!
Heaven = Jesus' glory place.
Heaven is Glory Land.

Who Is a Citizen?

Look up the word *citizen* in a dictionary. What does it mean to be a citizen of your country or town? What are some things a good citizen says and does? Who are some good citizens that you know? What makes them good citizens? Write or tell your answers to one another. Or draw pictures of people acting as good citizens and make a booklet.

Good Citizen Coupons

Make coupons to give to others for being good citizens in the school, family, and community. Perhaps the coupons are favorite Bible verses or they can be redeemed for a special treat. In Christ's family, though, we can't do anything to earn our citizenship. Our Savior has done it all for us by dying on the cross and taking our sins away. God gives us the power to be His Easter people and Christian citizens. He gives us citizenship in our heavenly home for Jesus' sake.

Citizen Badges

To the teacher: If your church or school has one, children will enjoy using a commercial button maker for this activity.

Make badges to declare that you are a heavenly citizen. Cut circles from poster board, use marking pens to decorate them, and add self-adhesive pin backs. Wear your badges happily and proudly as you witness to Jesus' faith family of citizens.

Heavenly Name Book

Citizens—taxpayers and voters—have their names written into their town's record books. When we are baptized, our names are recorded in the church record books. Best of all, we can be happy and thankful that God has written our names into His book in heaven!

Ask everyone to make a page for a special book. First, punch three holes into a sheet of construction paper. Write your name on the paper using large letters. Use gold, silver, or brightly colored plastic jewels to decorate your name. Or write your name with a glitter pen. When your page is dry, use thick yarn or gold cord to tie it with the others into a book. Use your heavenly name book as a reminder that God has written your names into His heavenly book and promises to take you there!

Make a Heavenly Dessert

Work together to peel four oranges. Divide them into thin slices and place in a bowl. Peel one banana, cut it into thin slices, and add it to the bowl. Blend ½ cup orange juice, ¼ cup honey, and 2 tablespoons lemon juice. Pour the mixture over the fruit. Sprinkle with coconut. *(Makes four servings.)*

Celebrate Inheritance

Scripture to Read:

Leviticus 20:24; Numbers 26:52–56; Joshua 11:23; Psalm 33:12; 136:21–22; Matthew 25:34; Ephesians 1:13–14, 18–20; Colossians 3:23–24; 1 Peter 1:3–4

Bible Stories to Learn:

Jacob Gets Isaac's Blessing (Genesis 27:1–28:5); Jesus Teaches the Beatitudes (Matthew 5:1–16)

Books to Read about Inheritance:

Adopted and Loved Forever (CPH, 56–1624)

God's Word to Remember:

[Jesus says,] "Come, you who are blessed by My Father; take your inheritance, the kingdom prepared for you since the creation of the world." *Matthew 25:34*

We are God's children. Now if we are children, then we are heirs—heirs of God and co-heirs with Christ, if indeed we share in His sufferings in order that we may also share in His glory. *Romans 8:16–17*

Set Up Your Center

As the focal point, use a large cardboard box with a lid. Cut along three sides of one panel so the top will open as if hinged. Cover the box with foil wrapping paper to look like a treasure box. Tape a card to the side of the treasure box that reads **Our Inheritance.**

Inside the box, place smaller boxes of various sizes. In each smaller container, place the directions and materials for the activities you selected. Wrap each container in bright wrapping paper.

Activities

What Is an *Inheritance*?

Look up *inheritance* in a dictionary. Then read some or all of the suggested Bible readings. Write a short definition of *inheritance* in your own words.

Needs, Wants, and God's Gifts

Read the Bible story of Jesus visiting Mary and Martha (Luke 10:38–42). What do you think Jesus meant when He said, "But only one thing is *needed*. Mary has chosen what is better, and it will not be taken away from her"?

Label each of three paper grocery bags **Needs, Wants,** and **God's Gifts.** Cut pictures from magazines of things that we need to live (or draw pictures of items on separate sheets of paper). Place them in the **Needs** bag. Cut pictures from magazines of

INHERITANCE CENTER

things that you want (or draw pictures of items on separate sheets of paper). Place them in the **Wants** bag. Cut pictures from magazines of God's gifts to us (or draw pictures of items on separate sheets of paper). Place them in the **God's Gifts** bag. Which bag is most important for your life? Why? Thank God for giving you the one thing "needed" in life—your inheritance as His dear child: *salvation through Jesus Christ.*

41

UNFOLDING STORY

Read the Bible story about Jacob receiving his brother, Esau's, blessing (Genesis 27:1–28:5). Why did Jacob trick his father, Isaac? Read more about birthrights and blessings in a Bible commentary.

Draw each part of the Bible story on a different sheet of paper. Tape the papers together in the correct order to make a book. Use it to retell the story, showing your illustrations to your family and friends.

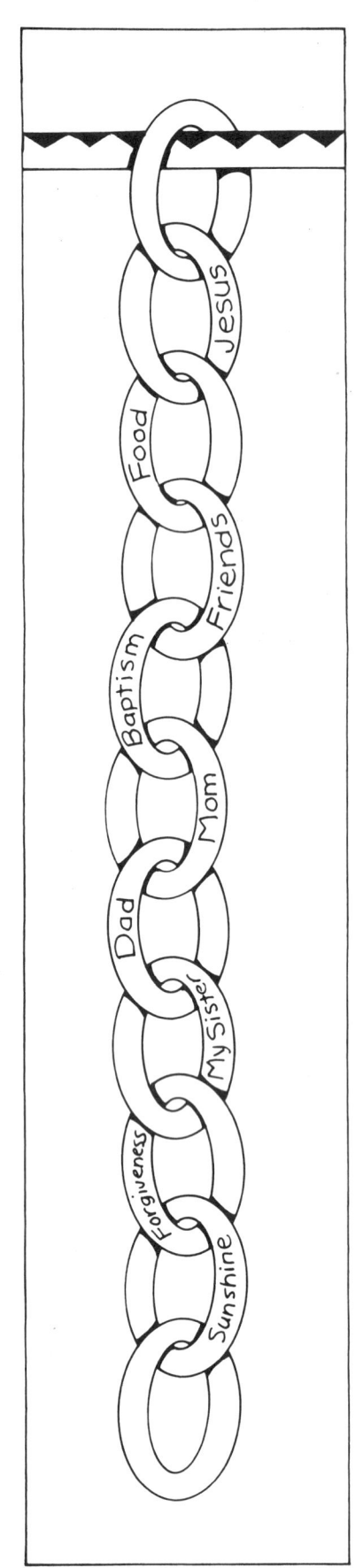

BLESSINGS CHAIN

God's love is like a circle—it has no beginning and it has no end. Cut construction paper into strips. Use a marking pen to write one of God's blessings to you on each strip. On other strips, write short thank-You prayers to God for blessings such as making you His child, your Baptism, Jesus' saving action, forgiveness, and for the many ways He loves and cares for you each day. Link the strips together into a chain. Hang the colorful chain where it can remind you of the inheritance God gives you and that His love never ends.

TREE OF LIFE

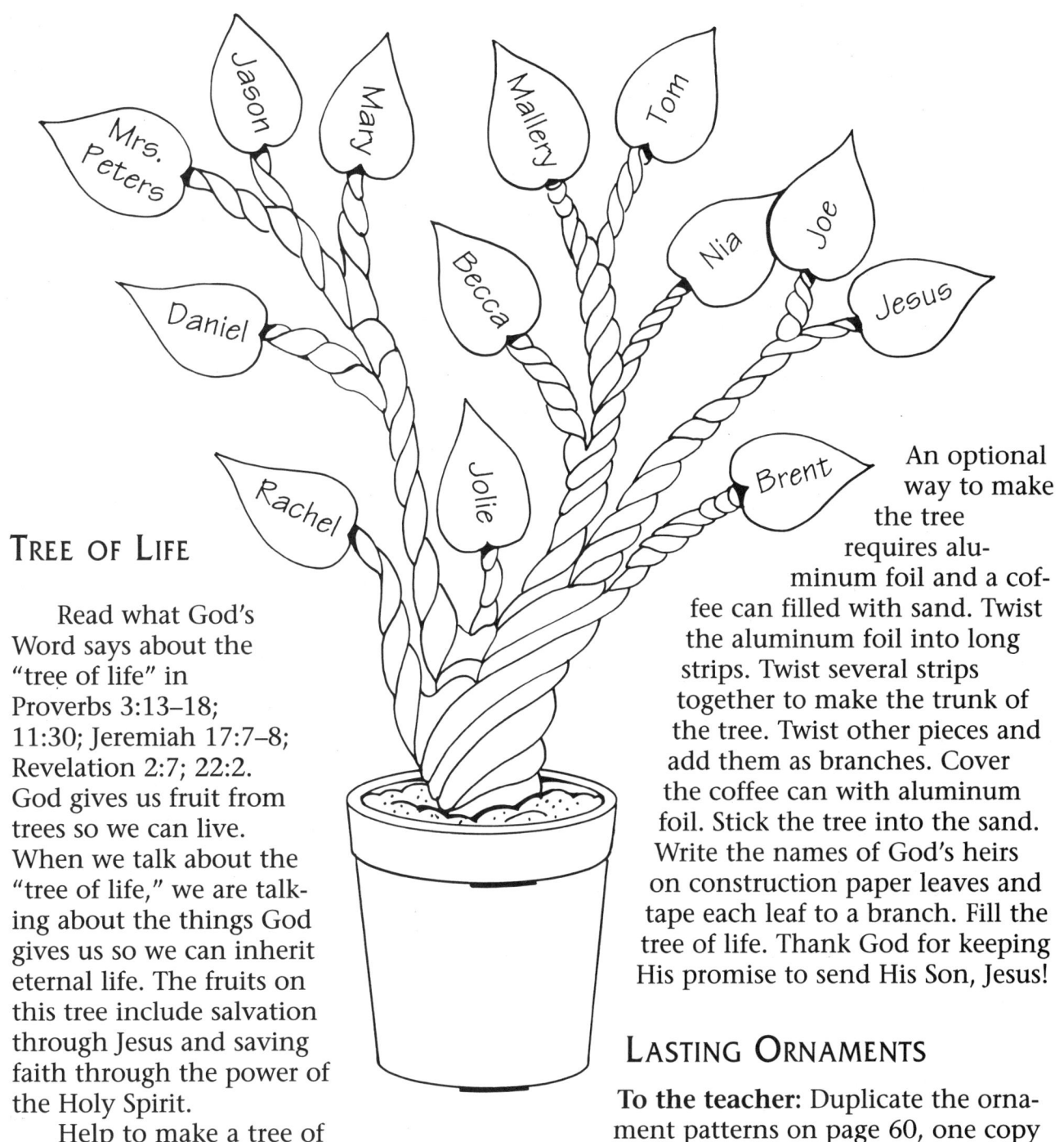

Read what God's Word says about the "tree of life" in Proverbs 3:13–18; 11:30; Jeremiah 17:7–8; Revelation 2:7; 22:2. God gives us fruit from trees so we can live. When we talk about the "tree of life," we are talking about the things God gives us so we can inherit eternal life. The fruits on this tree include salvation through Jesus and saving faith through the power of the Holy Spirit.

Help to make a tree of life as a visual reminder of God's blessings to you as His heirs of salvation. Hang butcher paper on a wall. Use tempera paint to paint a tree on the paper. Let dry. Add construction paper leaves to the tree with the names of Jesus and everyone in your class. You also can add the names of others who are heirs of Christ's gift of heaven.

An optional way to make the tree requires aluminum foil and a coffee can filled with sand. Twist the aluminum foil into long strips. Twist several strips together to make the trunk of the tree. Twist other pieces and add them as branches. Cover the coffee can with aluminum foil. Stick the tree into the sand. Write the names of God's heirs on construction paper leaves and tape each leaf to a branch. Fill the tree of life. Thank God for keeping His promise to send His Son, Jesus!

LASTING ORNAMENTS

To the teacher: Duplicate the ornament patterns on page 60, one copy for each child.

Cut ornaments from construction paper or poster board. Use marking pens, craft paint, or glitter pens to decorate the ornaments. Include crosses, flowers, butterflies, candles, sunshine, rainbows, and words or phrases such as **Heaven, Jesus Saves,** and **God Is Love.** Hang your ornaments on the tree of life you made.

CELEBRATE JESUS

SCRIPTURE TO READ:
John 3:16; Acts 16:31; 1 Corinthians 8:6

GOD'S WORD TO REMEMBER:
Believe in the Lord Jesus, and you will be saved. *Acts 16:31*

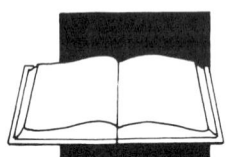

BIBLE STORIES TO LEARN:
Jesus Is Born (Luke 2:1–20); The Boy Jesus Visits the Temple (Luke 2:41–52); John Baptizes Jesus (Matthew 3:13–17); Jesus Loves All People (Luke 19:1–10); Jesus Gives Us His Supper (Luke 22:7–20); Jesus Dies and Comes Alive (Luke 23:26–24:12); Jesus Returns to Heaven (Acts 1:1–11); Jesus Will Come Again (Matthew 28:16–20; Revelation 22:20)

BOOKS TO READ ABOUT JESUS:
God Promised Us a Savior (CPH, 59–1442); *Baby Jesus Is Born* (CPH, 59–1467); *Baby Jesus, Prince of Peace* (CPH, 59–1471); *The Story of Jesus' Baptism and Temptation* (CPH, 59–1503); *Zacchaeus* (CPH, 59–1460); *Jesus and the Grumpy Little Man* (CPH, 59–1482); *The Bread and the Wine* (CPH, 59–1245); *The Very First Lord's Supper* (CPH, 59–1501); *Good Friday* (CPH, 59–1451); *The Day Jesus Died* (CPH, 59–1516); *My Happy Easter Book* (CPH, 59–1493); *The Easter Women* (CPH, 59–1431); *The Story of the Empty Tomb* (CPH, 59–1512); *Jesus Returns to Heaven* (CPH, 59–1476)

SET UP YOUR CENTER

Cover a table with a colorful plastic or paper tablecloth. Paint **We celebrate Jesus!** on the sides. Add colorful squiggles, stars, flowers, and balloons. Let dry. Place a picture of Jesus in the center of the table. Anchor several colorful helium-filled balloons next to it. Hang crepe paper streamers above the table.

Place containers of various sizes covered in festive wrapping paper on or around the "Jesus" table. Place the directions and materials for the activities you chose inside the containers. On each container, attach a picture of Jesus' happy face.

ACTIVITIES

WHO IS JESUS? TREASURE HUNT

Read Bible stories about Jesus and the ways He showed love to others. Think about words and phrases that answer the question "Who is Jesus?" Write your answers on slips of construction paper. Hide the strips of paper, as well as objects such as a small cross, a plastic egg, a small lamb, a heart, a seashell, and any other thing that reminds you of Jesus. Ask your friends to look for the papers and objects

Jesus Center

We celebrate Jesus!

in a set amount of time. Show one another what you have found and talk about how much Jesus loves you.

I See Jesus!

To the teacher: Duplicate the eyeglasses pattern on page 59, one for each child. Enlarge or reduce as needed.

Use the pattern to cut a pair of eyeglasses from poster board. Tape small squares of colored cellophane over each eyehole. When you look through the glasses, you'll see everything in color. As you wear your glasses, think about ways that you "see Jesus" in the world—in people's words and actions, in the beauty of nature, as you forgive one another.

Jesus Weaving

Did you know that the Asante *(a SAN tay)* people in Ghana, Africa, make a beautiful cloth once worn only by kings? It's called kente *(KEN tay)* cloth. The cloth makers cut strips from fine rayon or silk and sew them together in colorful patterns. People hang the fabric on a wall or use it to make clothes.

You can make a "Jesus weaving" to hang on your wall to remind you that God sent Jesus to be your Savior and King. Fold a 12" × 18" sheet of dark purple construction paper in half. Start at the fold and cut 1" wide slits, stopping about 2" from the edge of the paper. Open the paper. Cut 1" × 12" strips of construction paper using bright colors. Weave each strip in and out of the slits you cut into the purple paper. Start row 1 by going under, over, under, over until the end. Start row 2 by going over, under, over, under until the end. Continue alternating the strips.

Use marking pens or glitter pens to write words on your weaving such as

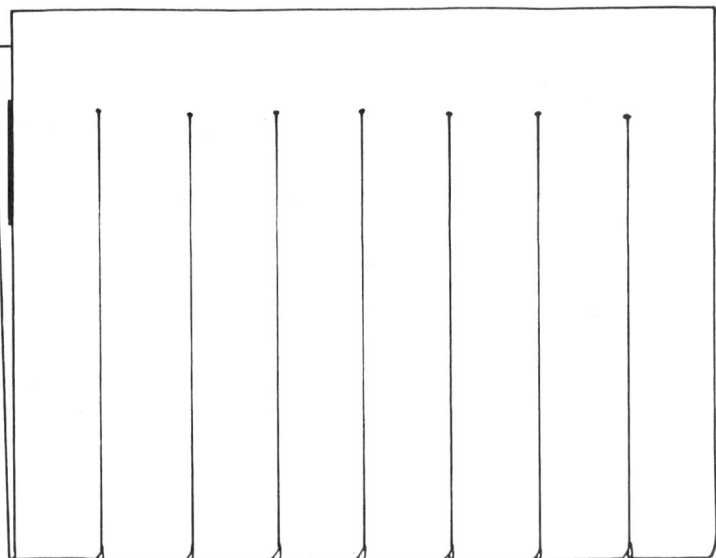

J-E-S-U-S

Jesus is our King.

Jesus is King in our home.

We love Jesus.

You also might want to make a paper weaving for each member of your family. Write table prayers on the weaving that include your thanks to Jesus for being your Savior and King. Cover each weaving with clear adhesive paper to make place mats.

Jesus Gift

Many people have never heard of Jesus. They don't know who He is or what He has done for all people. They don't celebrate His love and forgiveness in their everyday lives. How will they know Jesus if someone does not tell them? (Romans 10:17)

Collect boxes of various sizes—jewelry boxes, shoe boxes, cereal boxes, tissue boxes, and small appliance boxes. Gather colorful wrapping paper and ribbons. Make note cards from construction paper. Draw pictures and add stickers, glitter paint, buttons, lace, and ribbon. Write messages that tell the Good News about Jesus on the inside of the cards. Put the messages in the boxes and wrap them. You might include a Gospel tract, a Bible, a picture book, or a brochure that tells about Jesus and His love. Give the message gift to someone who needs to hear about Jesus.

Jesus' Names

List as many names as you can for Jesus. Use your Bible to help you. Draw your own picture of Jesus and use some of the names to write a caption that explains who Jesus is.

Jesus and Me

To the teacher: Duplicate the cube pattern on page 61, one for each child.

Jesus is our best Friend. He is always with us. He wants us to talk with Him in prayer. He hears us and promises to answer us. We can always trust Jesus.

Trace the cube pattern on a sheet of poster board or construction paper. Cut it out. Write Jesus' name and draw a picture of Him in one square. Write your name and draw a picture of yourself in another square. Add other pictures or stickers and decorations to the remaining squares.

Fold in the outside edges of the square and tape your cube together. Keep it as a reminder of your Savior, Jesus, and His love for you.

Jesus Puppet

Make a Jesus puppet to use when you tell favorite Bible stories to your friends and family. Set a paper lunch bag on the table with the folded bottom right-side up. Draw eyes, nose, and mouth on the bottom section. Glue brown yarn to the bag for hair and a beard. Draw clothes on your Jesus puppet.

You also can make other lunch bag puppets to represent Jesus' friends; His mother, Mary; Zacchaeus; and your friends or family members. Use the puppets to tell Bible stories that show Jesus sharing His love and forgiveness with people.

Celebrate Kingdom

Scripture to Read:

Daniel 4:3; 7:27;
Matthew 6:33; 13:31–32;
Matthew 16:19; 19:14;
25:34; Romans 14:17

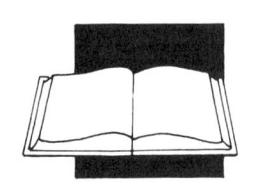

Bible Stories to Learn:

Jesus Teaches Us to Pray (Matthew 6:5–13); Jesus Takes Care of His Children (Matthew 6:25–34; 18:1–6; 19:13–15); Kingdom Parables (Matthew 13:31–50); Jesus Saves Zacchaeus (Luke 19:1–10); Jesus Will Take Us to Heaven (Matthew 25:31–46; 28:16–20)

Books to Read about Kingdom:

The Lord's Prayer (CPH, 59-1459); *The Day the Little Children Came* (CPH, 59-1210); *Jesus Blesses the Little Children* (CPH, 59-1500); *Jesus and the Little Children* (CPH, 59-1481); *Zacchaeus* (CPH, 59-1460); *Jesus and the Grumpy Little Man* (CPH, 59-1482)

God's Word to Remember:

[Jesus] has made us to be a kingdom and priests to serve His God and Father. *Revelation 1:6*

Since we are receiving a kingdom that cannot be shaken, let us be thankful. *Hebrews 12:28*

You will receive a rich welcome into the eternal kingdom of our Lord and Savior Jesus Christ. *2 Peter 1:11*

Set Up Your Center

Use a large refrigerator or freezer box to make a castle. Cut out the bottom of the box and tape the top shut with duct tape. Tape an oatmeal box to each corner. Form a cone "turret" from construction paper and tape one to the top of each oatmeal box. Cut rounded windows in each of the three sides and a rounded castle door in the fourth side. Use marking pens, paint, fabric, and anything else to decorate the castle.

Label plastic laundry baskets or boxes **Kingdom Kids**. Place the directions and materials for the activities you selected inside these containers. Set the containers around the castle.

Activities

What Is a Kingdom?

Look up the word *kingdom* in a dictionary. Write your own short description for the word. Then look up *animal kingdom* and *plant kingdom* in a science book or encyclopedia. God has created many different kingdoms in His world, hasn't He?

Think about God's spiritual kingdom—the family of believers both here on earth

Kingdom Center

and in heaven. Read 1 Chronicles 29:11, Matthew 6:33, and John 3:3–5. Read some of the other suggested Bible verses about God's kingdom. List what you discover about God's kingdom.

Build Your Own Kingdom

Collect small boxes and recyclable containers of all shapes and sizes. Work alone or with friends to build a creative kingdom. Use duct tape, masking tape, or glue to attach the boxes to one another. You could make a castle or a town or a maze. Name your kingdom. Decorate your kingdom. Write a story about who lives in your kingdom. You also could use aluminum cans; flexible foam pieces; sugar cubes and white glue; sand or snow; or wooden blocks and scraps of wood to build your kingdom.

Keys to God's Kingdom

To the teacher: Duplicate the key patterns on page 62, several for each child.

Make a key chain to remind you of the kingdom God has prepared for you through Jesus. Use the pattern to cut keys from construction paper. Punch a hole in the end of each key. Lace cord or yarn through the keys and tie a knot. Read the Bible verses listed below and write your favorite verses on the keys.

God's Kingdom Family Tree

Read the Bible verses about God's kingdom. List all the people you know who are in God's kingdom through their Baptism and faith in Jesus. Draw and color a big tree on a large sheet of construction paper or poster board. Add the names of people from your list to the tree. Use a different color to write some of God's blessings on the tree.

Exodus 15:2

Psalm 95:1–3

Psalm 118:1

Isaiah 60:16

Matthew 5:1–12

Matthew 6:10

Matthew 7:7–8

John 14:1–12

John 14:6

Acts 10:43

1 John 3:2

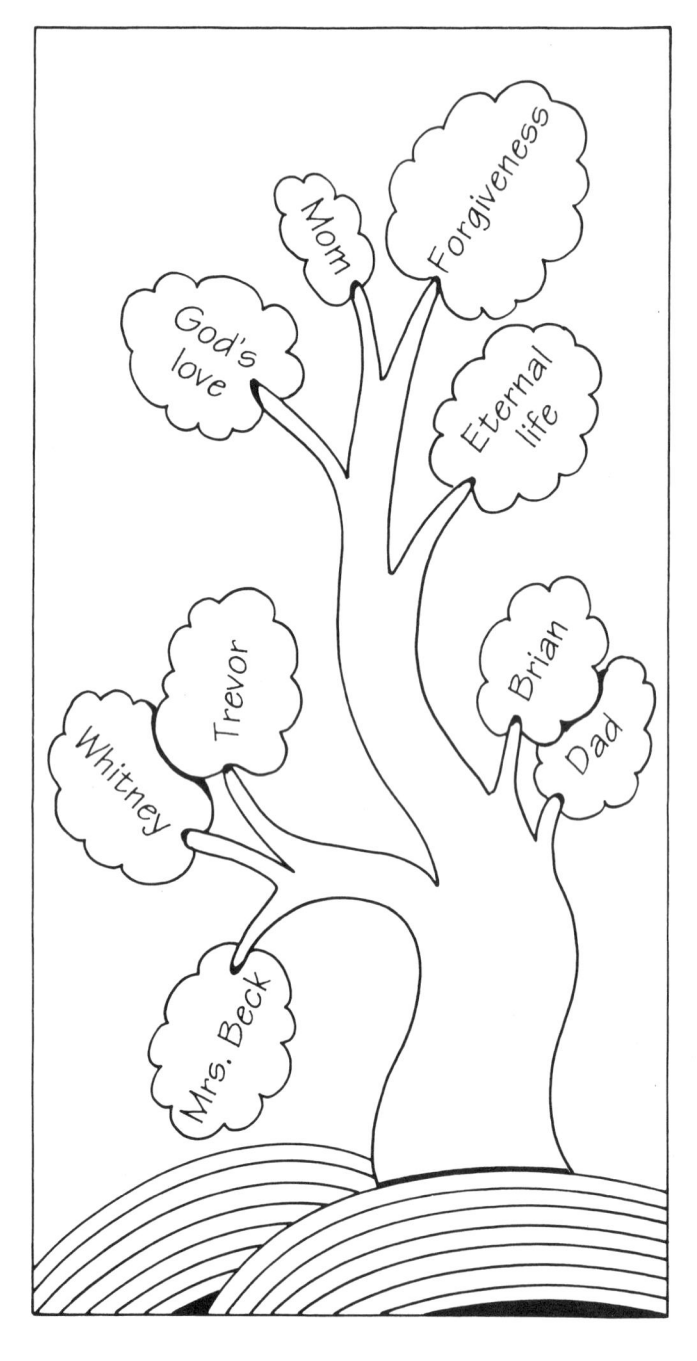

KINGDOM QUILT BLOCKS

To the teacher: Cut paper squares of equal size, one for each child.

Work together to make a kingdom quilt. Use marking pens, crayons, pencils, glue, glitter, or collage materials to decorate your square. Glue the completed squares to a large sheet of butcher paper or to a vinyl tablecloth. Hang it on the wall under a banner that says **Kids of the Kingdom.**

BIBLE VERSE FLIP-FLOPS

Make flip-flops to help you and your friends memorize special Bible verses. Fold a 12" × 18" sheet of construction paper in half. Then fold it into fourths. Open the paper and lay it horizontally on the table. Cut along each of the four lines, starting at the bottom and stopping on the center fold. Refold the paper. Choose a Bible verse about God's kingdom. Write the Bible verse in the squares that are not cut, putting some words in each section. Then draw simple pictures that represent the words in the squares on the flaps. Look at the pictures and try to remember the Bible words underneath. Open the flaps to peek at the words.

CELEBRATE LEADERS

SCRIPTURE TO READ:

Psalm 23:2; Matthew 6:13; John 10:2–5; Galatians 3:24; Revelation 7:17

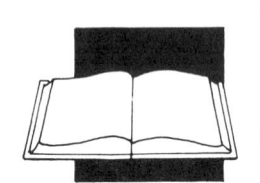

BIBLE STORIES TO LEARN:

God Leads Noah and His Family to Safety (Genesis 6:1–9:17); God Leads His People Out of Egypt (Exodus 12:31–15:21); God Gives Victory at Jericho (Joshua 5:13–6:25); God Uses Deborah to Save Canaan (Judges 4:1–5:31); God Uses Gideon to Defeat the Midianites (Judges 6:1–7:25); God Gives Leaders to Israel (1 Samuel 3:1–21; 8:1–11:15; 16:1–13; 2 Samuel 1:1–6:23); God Helps Esther Save Her People (The Book of Esther); Our Good Shepherd Cares for Us (John 10:1–18)

BOOKS TO READ ABOUT LEADERS:

The Story of Noah's Ark (CPH, 59-1110); *Noah and God's Promises* (CPH, 59-1294); *Noah's Floating Zoo* (CPH, 59-1464); *Moses and the Freedom Flight* (CPH, 59-1478); *Journey to the Promised Land* (CPH, 59-1484); *The Fall of Jericho* (CPH, 59-1473); *Samuel and the Wake-Up Call* (CPH, 59-1458); *David and Goliath* (CPH, 59-1457); *The Boy with a Sling* (CPH, 59-1116); *David and the Dreadful Giant* (CPH, 59-1483); *The Queen Who Saved Her People* (CPH, 59-1194); *Jesus the Good Shepherd* (CPH, 59-1441)

GOD'S WORD TO REMEMBER:

Teach me Your way, O Lord; lead me in a straight path. *Psalm 27:11*

SET UP YOUR CENTER

Make a dimensional "leader" to hang from the ceiling. First, cut two large people shapes from newsprint, butcher paper, or poster board. Staple the two shapes together around the head and shoulders. Stuff wads of newspaper between the two shapes, stuffing and stapling all the way to the feet. Add facial features and hair. Keep the rest of the figure generic. Print **Leader** on a wide ribbon the figure wears diagonally like a sash.

Under the leader, place colorful plastic storage crates. Each crate holds directions and materials needed to complete an activity of your choice.

ACTIVITIES

MAKE A LINE OF LEADERS

What does a leader do? How does he or she lead others? Who are the leaders in your class? in your family? in your church? in your community? in your state and country?

Cut "cookie cutter" people from construction paper. Write the name of one leader on each paper person. Then write a

Leaders Center

short phrase or sentence that tells what this leader does. Use clothespins to clip all the leaders to a clothesline stretched across the corner of the room. Thank God for the leaders whom you know and for their special work.

Design a Leader Stamp

Important leaders often are pictured on special stamps called *commemorative* stamps. Every time someone uses the stamp on a letter, the leader is remembered.

Design your own commemorative stamp for a leader. First, choose one of the suggested Bible stories and read about a leader God helped. Why did the people need a leader? How did God choose the leader? What was God's action in the Bible story? Use marking pens and crayons to design a commemorative stamp on a sheet of paper that shows what one of God's leaders in the Bible did to help others.

Then think of one of your favorite leaders. How does God help that leader? Design a stamp that shows your favorite leader and why that leader is important. Thank God for all the leaders He gives us.

"Lead the Followers" Game

Play Follow the Leader. Choose someone to start the game as a leader whom everyone else follows. Change leaders often, allowing each child to have a turn. Think of fun, creative things to do when you are the leader. Jump up, holding something between your knees; twirl around; wiggle your ears; wave; take off your shoe and hop on one foot; open your Bible; pretend to nap; give someone a hug.

Jesus, Our Good Shepherd

To the teacher: Duplicate the sheep and shepherd patterns on page 64, one for each child. (You may want to duplicate extra sheep patterns for each child.)

Read John 10:1–18. Who is the leader in this Bible story? What does the leader do? Who are the followers? What do they do? What special quality do the followers recognize in their leader? How do we recognize our leader Jesus in our daily lives? How do we follow Jesus?

Use the patterns to cut out a shepherd and some sheep. Write your answers to the questions on each of the shapes. Keep them where they will help you remember that Jesus, our Good Shepherd, leads us and supplies us with everything we need.

Pop-up Card

To the teacher: Duplicate the pop-up card pattern on page 63, one for each child.

Cut out the pattern to make your own thank-you cards for leaders you know. Decorate the outside of the cards. Write a special thank-you note or draw a fun picture on the pop-up section of the card. Add a favorite Bible verse on the inside of the card. Fold along the dotted lines, folding down the pop-up section to go inside the card. Give the cards to leaders such as your parents, grandparents, pastors, teachers, youth workers, special neighbors, or the mayor.

Celebrate Music

Scripture to Read:

Judges 5:3; Psalm 27:6; 57:7; 92:1–4; Ephesians 5:19–20

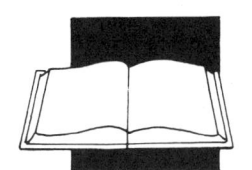

Bible Stories to Learn:

The Song of Moses and Miriam (Exodus 15:1–21); God Helps Joshua at Jericho (Joshua 6:1–25); David Serves Saul (1 Samuel 16:14–23); The Angels Sing Praises (Luke 2:8–14); Jesus Enters Jerusalem (Matthew 21:1–11); Paul and Silas Sing Praises (Acts 16:16–34)

Books to Read about Music:

The Fall of Jericho (CPH, 59–1473); *The Night the Angels Sang* (CPH, 59–1213); *Jesus Enters Jerusalem* (CPH, 59–1455)

God's Word to Remember:

Sing to God, sing praise to His name. *Psalm 68:4*

Set Up Your Center

Cut large, colorful musical notes from poster board or construction paper. Tape them to the outsides of plastic crates or boxes. On one container, tape a sheet of paper that reads **Celebrate Music!** In each crate or box, place the materials and directions for the activities you selected. Place the crates or boxes on a rolling cart to move freely around your room.

Activities

Produce a Mini-musical

The following musicals can help reinforce Scripture.
- "Man Overboard!" (Narrative of Jonah through song) by Jeffrey E. Burkart (CPH, 97–6521).
- "Noah's RemARKable Voyage" by John Folkening (CPH, 97–6108)
- "The Summer Solution" by John Folkening (CPH, 97–6210)

Check your local Christian bookstore for additional musicals based on Scripture. Work together to produce the musical. Use it as an opportunity to share God's Word with others in addition to offering entertainment.

Rhythm Instruments

Gather donated items such as oatmeal boxes, blocks of wood, dowel rods, sandpaper, Chinet dinner plates, rubber bands,

Music Center

twist ties, soda can tabs, yarn, and beans or rice. Use these items to make simple drums, shakers, tambourines, sandpaper blocks, wood blocks, and rhythm sticks to use while you sing praises to God.

Musical Parade

Provide a tape player or CD player with good batteries. Play favorite audiocassettes or compact discs of Bible story and Gospel songs for a sing-along. Move to the music. You can sway, dance, hop, twirl, jump, etc. Wave colorful scarves or ribbons to the beat. Play rhythm instruments with the music.

Make Note Cards

Make a card by folding a sheet of construction paper in half. Decorate the front of the card with musical notes and happy people. Use marking pens to write a message about the love of Jesus inside the card. Add stickers. Give your card to someone who is sick or needs to hear about Jesus' love.

Make Musical Cassette Cards

Use a blank audiocassette and a tape recorder to record a message about Jesus and His love. You could sing favorite songs, tell a Bible story in your own words, read a Bible storybook, or just tell why you love Jesus. Think about someone who needs to hear a cheerful message. Take your recording and listen to it together.

Oh, When the Saints Go Marchin' In

Did you know that you are a saint? Each believer in Jesus is a sinner and a saint at the same time. Read Colossians 1:2, 9–12. You are a sinner, but Jesus has made you a saint by dying for your sins on the cross. He gives you the golden crown and the glorious robe of His holiness to wear as one of God's redeemed, faithful people.

Think of yourself as a saint. List all the good things Jesus helps you do for other saints around you. Write **I am a saint. You are a saint. We are saints together.** at the top of your list. Keep the list handy to help you remember how you can share Jesus' love with other saints.

Pray a Hymn

Look in a hymnal or songbook to find a song that you could use as a prayer. List the songs or copy the verses into a prayer journal. Use one hymn or song stanza as you pray each day.

Write a New Song

Think of the melody to a song you like to sing. It could be "Twinkle, Twinkle Little Star," "The Farmer in the Dell," "Row, Row, Row Your Boat," or "Frere Jacques." Write your own words that tell how much you love Jesus to sing to the melody. Sing your song for your friends or your family. Have others sing their song to you.

This Little Gospel Light of Mine

Make large paper candles by taping construction paper around paper towel tubes. Add a flame to the top cut from yellow or orange paper. Hold your candles as you sing "This Little Gospel Light of Mine."

Favorite Songs Video

Make a videotape of favorite "Jesus" songs. Sing, do actions, and move to the music. Use puppets and say favorite Bible verses between songs too. Make copies of the videotape and give them as gifts.

Resurrection Sun Cross

Paper Egg People Messengers

I See Jesus! Eyeglasses

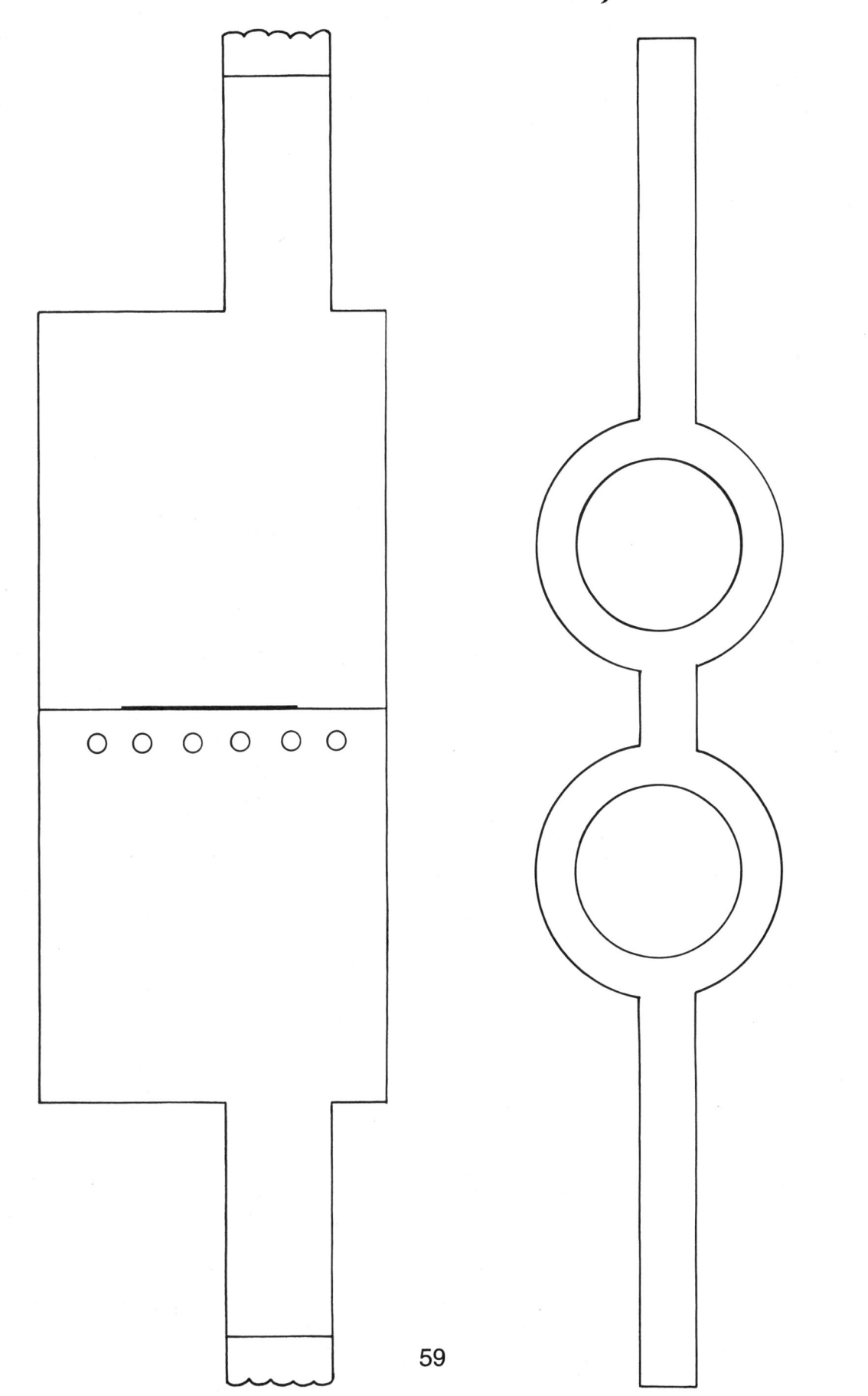

59

LASTING ORNAMENTS

Jesus and Me Cube

61

Key Patterns

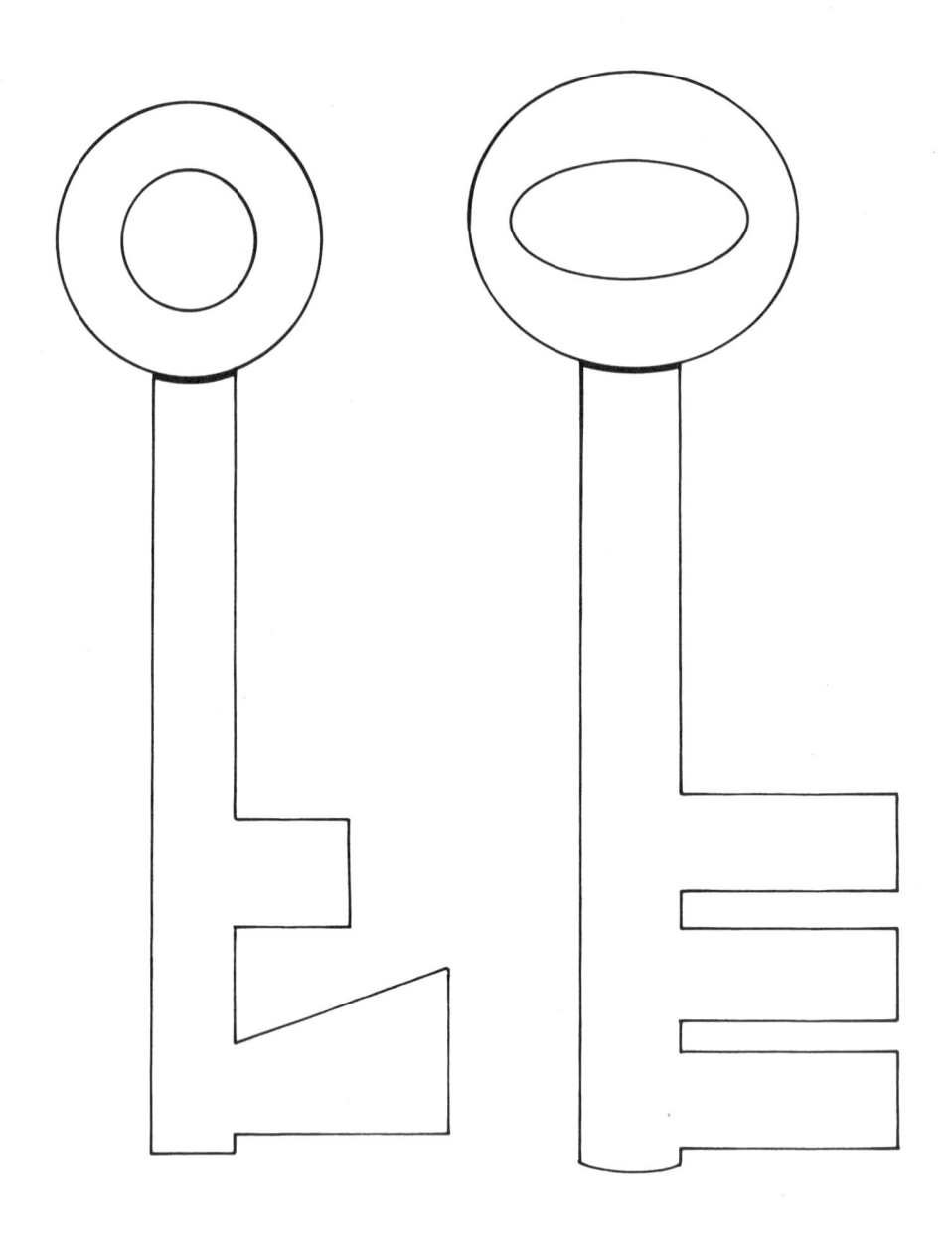

Pop-up Card

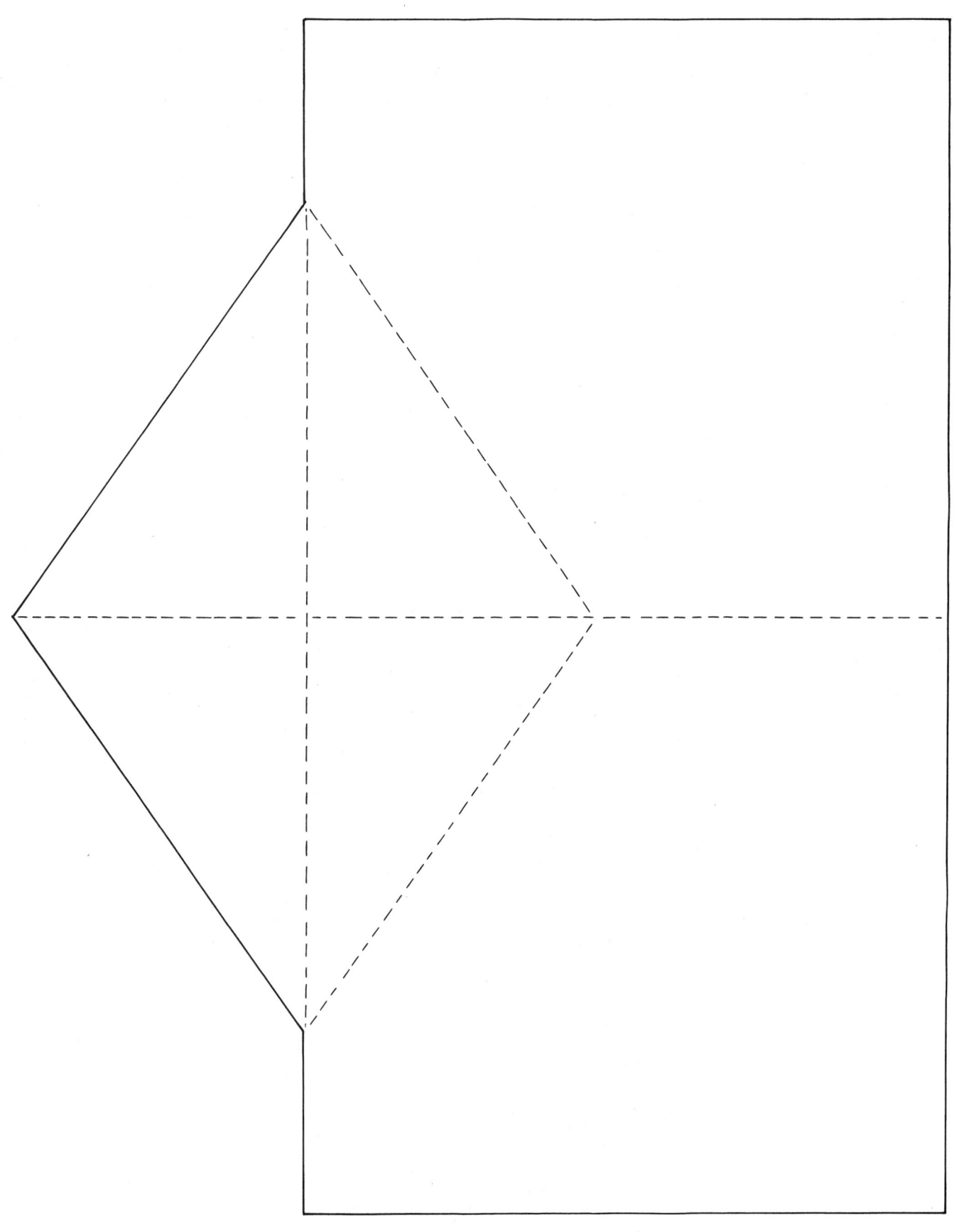

Jesus, Our Good Shepherd Patterns